Berlitz®

Nordic
Europe

phrase book & dictionary

Berlitz Publishing
New York   London   Singapore

Contacting the Editors
Every effort has been made to provide accurate information in this publication, but changes are inevitable. The publisher cannot be responsible for any resulting loss, inconvenience or injury. We would appreciate it if readers would call our attention to any errors or outdated information. We also welcome your suggestions; if you come across a relevant expression not in our phrase book, please contact us at: **comments@berlitzpublishing.com**

All Rights Reserved
© 2019 Apa Digital (CH) AG and Apa Publications (UK) Ltd.
Berlitz Trademark Reg. U.S. Patent Office and other countries. Marca Registrada. Used under license from Berlitz Investment Corporation.

Printed in China

Editor: Zara Sekhavati
Translation: updated by Wordbank
Cover Design: Rebeka Davies
Interior Design: Beverley Speight
Picture Researcher: Beverley Speight
Cover Photos: Shutterstock
Interior Photos: iStockphoto 1, 13, 14, 21, 26, 28, 38, 42, 44, 45, 48, 81, 82, 153, 154, 157, 160, 189, 198, 214; David Hall 6, 9, 10, 17, 18, 24, 27, 31, 32, 36, 39, 40, 102, 104, 105, 131, 132, 200; Britta Jachinski 20, 67; Beverley Speight 22, 46, 69, 73, 75, 80, 101, 103, 130, 152, 155, 183, 188, 207, 211, 212; Ming Tang Evans 29, 35, 74; Yadid Levy 41; Gregory Wrona 43, 83, 85, 100, 170-181, 191, 192, 195, 197, 204, 205, 206, 208, 209; Julian Love 60, 63, 64, 76, 77, 79, 86, 87, 88, 91, 92, 95, 96, 97, 99; Richard Nowitz 70; Corrie Wingate 84, 120; Glyn Genin 116, 119, 127, 128, 135, 136, 137, 139, 140, 141, 143, 144, 146, 147, 148, 150, 151; Mina Patria 187; Tim Thompson 203, 210; Chris Stowles 202; William Shaw 201

Distribution

UK, Ireland and Europe
Apa Publications (UK) Ltd
sales@insightguides.com
United States and Canada
Ingram Publisher Services
ips@ingramcontent.com
Australia and New Zealand
Woodslane
info@woodslane.com.au
Southeast Asia
Apa Publications (SN) Pte

singaporeoffice@insightguides.com
Worldwide
Apa Publications (UK) Ltd
sales@insightguides.com

Special Sales, Content Licensing, and CoPublishing
Discounts available for bulk quantities. We can create special editions, personalized jackets, and corporate imprints. sales@insightguides.com; www.insightguides.biz

Contents

How to use this Book

> Sometimes you see two alternatives separated by a slash. Choose the one that's right for your situation.

ESSENTIAL

I'm here on vacation [holiday]/business.

Jeg er her på ferie/forretningsrejse. *yie ehr hehr paw fehr·yer/foh·reht·nings·rie·ser*

I'm going to...

Jeg skal til... *yie skal til...*

I'm staying at the... Hotel.

Jeg bor på Hotel... *yie boar paw hoa·tehl...*

> Words you may see are shown in YOU MAY SEE boxes.

YOU MAY SEE...

TOLD	customs
TOLDFRIE VARER	duty-free goods
VARER AT ANGIVE	goods to declare

> Any of the words or phrases listed can be plugged into the sentence below.

At the Hotel

Does the hotel have...?

Har hotellet...? *hah hoa·tehl·erdh...*

a computer

en pc *ehn peh seh*

an elevator [a lift]

en elevator *ehn eh·ler·va·toh*

(wireless) internet

(trådløst) internet *(trowdh·lurst) in·tah·neht*

room service

service på værelset *sur·vees paw vehrl·serdh*

Danish phrases appear in purple.

Read the simplified pronunciation as if it were English.

Relationships

I'm...	**Jeg er...** *yie ehr...*
married	**gift** *geefd*
divorced	**skilt** *skild*
I'm widowed.	**Jeg er enkemand** *m*/**enke** *f. yie ehr ehn•ker•man/ehn•ker*

For Numbers, see page 159.

Related phrases can be found by going to the page number indicated.

When different gender forms apply, the masculine form is followed by *m*; feminine by *f*

In Denmark, upon meeting, it is customary to shake hands for both men and women. Close friends (male-female/female- female) may give kisses on the cheeks. As a greeting, you could say **Går det godt?** (How's it going?) or **Hva så?** (What's up?). **Hej** (general greeting) in Danish is used both for hello or hi and bye.

Information boxes contain relevant country, culture and language tips.

Expressions you may hear are shown in You May Hear boxes.

YOU MAY HEAR...

Næste! *nehs•der*	Next!
Din billet/Dit pas, tak. *deen bee•lehd/deet pas tahk*	Your ticket/passport, please.

Color-coded side bars identify each section of the book.

Danish

YOU MAY SEE...

Denmark, Norway and Sweden all use the same name for their currency, but the value differs in each country. The **krone** (meaning 'crown', pronounced _kroa·ner_ and abbreviated **kr.** or **DKK**), is divided into 100 **øre** (pronounced _ur·er_).

Coins: 25 and 50 **øre**, 1, 2, 5, 10 and 20 **kroner**

Notes: 50, 100, 200, 500 and 1,000 **kroner**

I'd like to change dollars/pounds into kroner.	**Jeg vil gerne veksle nogle dollars/pund til kroner.** _yie vil gehr·ner vehks·ler noa·ler doh·lahs/poon til kroa·ner_
I want to cash a traveler's check [cheque].	**Jeg vil gerne indløse en rejsecheck.** _yie vil gehr·ner in·lur·ser ehn rie·ser·shehk_
Can I pay in cash?	**Kan jeg betale med kontant** _kan yie beh·ta·ler mehdh kon·tant_
Can I pay by credit card?	**Kan jeg betale med kreditkort?** _kan yie beh·ta·ler mehdh kreh·deet·kawd_

For Numbers, see page 8.

Getting Around

How do I get to town?	**Hvordan kommer jeg ind til byen?** *voar•dan kohm•ah yie in til bew•ern*
Where's…?	**Hvor er…?** *voar ehr…*
the airport	**lufthavnen** *loaft•hown•ern*
the train [railway] station	**togstationen** *tow•sta•shoa•nern*
the bus station	**busstationen** *boos•sta•shoa•nern*
the subway [under-ground] station	**metrostationen** *meh•troa•sta•shoan•nern*

14

Copenhagen's **Metro** (subway) is a clean, quick and convenient way to travel through the city. You can purchase a **rabatkort** (10-trip ticket) or a 24-hour or 72-hour **CPHCARD** (Copenhagen Card) for discounted fares. Tickets for the **Metro** are interchangeable with those for buses and trains. Tickets must be stamped on the platform before boarding. Note that traveling without a valid ticket may lead to a sizeable fine.

YOU MAY HEAR...

igeud _lee·er·oodh_	straight ahead
til venstre _til vehn·sdrah_	on the left
til højre _til hoi·ah_	on the right
på/rundt om hjørnet _paw/roundt ohm yur·nerdh_	on/around the corner
overfor... _ow·ah·foh..._	opposite...
bagved... _ba·vehdh..._	behind...
ved siden af... _vehdh see·dhern a..._	next to...
efter... _ehf·dah..._	after...
nord/syd _noar/sewdh_	north/south
øst/vest _ursd/vehsd_	east/west
ved trafiklyset _vedh trah·feeg·lew·serdh_	at the traffic light
ved vejkrydset _vehdh vie·krew·serdh_	at the intersection

How far is it?	**Hvor langt er der?** _voar lahngt ehr dehr_
Where can I buy tickets?	**Hvor køber man billetter?** _voar kur·ber man bee·leh·dah_
A one-way/return ticket.	**En enkeltbillet/returbillet.** _ehn·kerld·bee·lehd/reh·toor·bee·lehd_
How much?	**Hvor meget koster det?** _voar mie·erdh kohs·dah deh_
Which...?	**Hvilken...?** _vil·kern..._
gate	**gate** _gayd_
line	**tog** _tow_
platform	**perron** _peh·rohng_
Where can I get a taxi?	**Hvor kan jeg få en taxa?** _voar kan yie fow ehn tahk·sa_

Denmark is comprised of some 500 islands. Though most of the larger islands are linked by bridges, ferries are a way of life in Denmark. There is regular local and international ferry service from Denmark to the Baltic States, England, Germany, Norway, Poland and Sweden. Passenger and car reservations can be made in advance via any travel agency.

Take me to this address.	**Kør mig til denne adresse.**	*kur mie til deh·ner a·drah·ser*
I would like to go to…Airport, please.	**Jeg vil gerne til… Lufthavn, tak.**	*yie vil gehr·ner til…loaft·hown tahk*
I'm in a rush.	**Jeg har travlt.** *yie har trowlt*	
Can I have a map?	**Har du et vejkort?** *har doo eht vie·kawd*	

Tickets

When's…to Århus?	**Hvornår afgår…til Århus?**	*voar·naw ow·gaw…til aw·hoos*
the first bus	**den første bus** *dehn fur·sder boos*	
the next flight	**det næste fly** *deh nehs·der flew*	
the last train	**det sidste tog** *deh sees·der tow*	
One ticket/Two tickets, please.	**En billet/To billetter, tak.**	*ehn bee·lehd/toa bee·leh·dah tahk*
For today/tomorrow.	**Til i dag/i morgen.** *til ee·dah/ee·mawn*	
A (an)…ticket.	**…billet.** *…bee·lehd*	
one-way [single]	**En enkelt** *ehn ehn·kerld*	
return trip	**En retur** *ehn reh·toor*	
first class	**En førsteklasse** *ehn furs·der kla·ser*	
I have an e-ticket.	**Jeg har en e-billet.** *yie har ehn eh·bee·lehd*	

DANSKE STATSBANER

The Danish train network connects towns across the main islands and the Jutland peninsula. Which train you choose depends on your destination and how quickly you want to get there. **S-bane** or **S-tog** is a commuter train, which serves Copenhagen and surrounding areas. Regional trains and **InterCity** (express) trains travel between Copenhagen and other parts of the country. The **Øresund** train connects Copenhagen and Malmö, Sweden.

A number of discounts are offered depending on the traveler (students, senior citizens, groups, families and children receive considerable reductions), day and time of travel (off-peak times are more highly discounted) as well as the destination. S-trains, the metro and buses run on an integrated network, so you may transfer without paying any additional cost. Keep in mind that buying a **rabatkort** (10-trip ticket), valid for a specified number of zones, is cheaper than buying single tickets. You may also want to consider a 24- hour or 72-hour **CPHCARD** (Copenhagen Card), which offers unlimited train, bus and metro transportation, free entry to over 60 museums and attractions and other discounts. The **CPHCARD** can be purchased online, at tourist offices, in the airport and at major train stations.

How long is the trip [journey]?	**Hvor længe tager turen?** *voar <u>layng</u>•er tah <u>too</u>•rern*
Is it a direct train?	**Er det et direkte tog?** *ehr deh ehd dee•reik•ter tow*
Can you tell me when to get off?	**Vil du sige til, når jeg skal af?** *vil doo <u>see</u>•yer til naw yie skal a*
I'd like to...my reservation.	**Jeg vil gerne...min bestilling.** *yie vil <u>gehr</u>•ner... meen beh•<u>stil</u>•ing*
cancel	**annullere** *<u>a</u>•noo•leh•rah*
change	**ændre** *<u>ehn</u>•drer*
confirm	**bekræfte** *beh•<u>krehf</u>•der*

For Time, see page 10.

Parking in Denmark is restricted. Metered zones allow up to three hours of parking. In Copenhagen, in unmetered zones, you will need to buy a ticket from a machine close by and display it on the dashboard of your car.

Taxis can be hailed in the street. Just look for the **FRI** (free) sign. Taxis can also be found at taxi stands, airports and train stations or booked over the phone. All cabs are metered and service charges are included in the fare, so tipping is not necessary. Most accept credit cards but be sure to check first.

Car Hire

Where can I hire a car?	**Hvor kan jeg leje en bil?** *voar kan yie lie•er ehn beel*
I'd like to hire…	**Jeg vil gerne leje…** *yie vil gehr•ner lie•er…*
a cheap/small car	**en billig/lille bil** *ehn bee•lee/lee•ler beel*
an automatic	**en bil med automatgear** *ehn beel mehdh ow•toa•mad geer*
a manual car	**almindeligt gear** *al•meen•deh•leet geer*
a car with air-conditioning	**en bil med klimaanlæg** *ehn beel medh klee•ma•an•layg*

Cycling is very much a part of daily life in Denmark and a regular means of transportation for many Danes. Great investment has been made in recent years to keep Copenhagen bike-friendly, prompting it to be labeled the 'City of Cyclists' of late. Bikes may be borrowed, free of charge, at one of the approximately 125 City Bike Parking spots around the city. All you have to do is leave a deposit that is returned to you when you bring the bike back to any City Bike Parking rack.

a car seat	**et barnesæde**	
	eht <u>bah</u>·ner·<u>say</u>·dher	
How much per day/ week?	**Hvad koster det per dag/uge?**	
	Vadh <u>kohs</u>·dah deh pehr da/<u>oo</u>·er	
Are there any discounts for…?	**Er der nogen specialtilbud…?**	
	ehr dehr <u>noa</u>·ern speh·<u>shal</u>·til·boodh…	

Places to Stay

Can you recommend a hotel?	**Kan du anbefale et hotel?**	
	kan doo <u>an</u>·beh·fa·ler eht hoa·<u>tehl</u>	
I have a reservation.	**Jeg har bestilt værelse.**	
	yie har beh·<u>stild</u> <u>vehrl</u>·ser	
My name is…	**Mit navn er…** *meet nown ehr…*	
Do you have a room…?	**Har I et værelse…?**	
	har ee ehd <u>vehrl</u>·ser…	
for one/two	**enkeltværelse/dobbeltværelse**	
	<u>ehn</u>·kerld·vehrl·ser/<u>doh</u>·berld·vehrl·ser	
with a bathroom	**med bad** *mehdh badh*	
with air-conditioning	**med klimaanlæg** *mehdh <u>klee</u>·ma·an·layg*	

for tonight	**for i nat** *for ee nad*
for two nights	**for to nætter** *for toa nay•dah*
for one week	**for en uge** *for ehn oo•er*
How much?	**Hvor meget koster det?** *voar mie•erdh kohs•dah deh*

In Denmark, there is a variety of places to stay in addition to hotels, which range from one to five stars. You could choose to stay in a bed and breakfast, such as a **kro** (country inn), in an old **slot** (castle) or a **motel** (motel). If you are traveling by car, good options include **vandrerhjem** (a hostel), **ungdomsherberg** (a student hotel) or **sommerhus** (a summer house), which refers to any rented living space, such as a seaside cottage or apartment. For a unique vacation experience, you might choose a **bondegårdsferie** (farmhouse stay), which lets you taste Danish farm life firsthand.
Advanced reservations are recommended particularly during the high season. If you arrive in Denmark without a reservation, tourist information offices can assist in locating places to stay as can the Room Reservation Service, found at Central Train Station in Copenhagen.

Do you have anything cheaper?	**Har du noget billigere?** *har doo noa•erdh bee•leer*
When's check-out?	**Hvornår skal vi tjekke ud?** *voar•naw skal vee tjeh•ker oodh*
Can I leave this in the safe?	**Må jeg lade dette være i boksen?** *mow yie la deh•ter vay•er i bohk•sern*
Can I leave my bags?	**Må jeg lade mine tasker være her?** *mow yie la mee•ner tas•gah vay•ah hehr*
Can I have the bill/ a receipt?	**Kan jeg få regningen/en kvittering?** *kan yie fow rie•ning•ern/ehn kvee•teh•ring*
I'll pay in cash/by credit card.	**Jeg vil gerne betale kontant/med kreditkort.** *yie vil gehr•ner beh•ta•ler kohn•tahnt/ mehdh kreh•deet•kawd*

Communications

Where's an internet cafe?	**Hvor ligger der en internetcafé?** *voar li•gah dehr ehn in•tah•neht•ca•feh*
Can I access the internet here/check my e-mail?	**Kan jeg gå på internettet herfra/tjekke min e-mail?** *kan yie gow paw in•tah•neh•derdh hehr•frah/tjay•ker meen ee•mail*

Danes tend to get right to business and don't engage in much small talk. When asked to give a briefing, be detailed, since Danes are rather meticulous. You'll find Danes to be comparatively serious and direct in business dealings and in their manner of speaking in general. This is not meant to insult. Though they are relatively informal, avoid comments that might be taken as personal.

How much per hour/half hour?	**Hvor meget koster det per time/halve time?** *voar mie•erdh kohs•dah deh pehr tee•mer/hal•ver tee•mer*
How do I connect/log on?	**Hvordan kobler/logger jeg mig på?** *voar •dan kohb•lah/lohg•ah yie mie paw*
I'd like a phone card, please.	**Jeg vil gerne have et telefonkort, tak.** *yie vil gehr•ner ha eht teh•ler•foan•kawd tahk*
Can I have your phone number?	**Kan jeg få dit telefonnummer?** *kan yie fow deet teh•ler•foan•noa•mer*
Here's my number/e-mail address.	**Her er mit telefonnumer/min e-mail-adresse.** *Hehr ehr meet teh•ler•foan•noa•mer/meen ee•mail•a•drah•ser*
Call me.	**Ring til mig.** *ring til mie*
Text me.	**Send mig venligst en tekstbesked.** *sehn mie vehn•leest ehn tehkst•beh•skehdh*
I'll text you.	**Jeg sender dig en tekstbesked.** *yie sehn•ah die ehn tehkst•beh•skehdh*
E-mail me.	**Send mig en e-mail.** *sehn mie ehn ee•mail*
Hello. This is...	**Hallo. Det er...** *ha•loa deh ehr...*

Brevene må ikke indeholde penge

POST

I'd like to speak to...	**Jeg vil gerne tale med...**	*yie vil <u>gehr</u>•ner <u>ta</u>•ler medh...*
Can you repeat that?	**Kan du gentage det?**	*kan doo <u>gehn</u>•ta deh*
I'll call back later.	**Jeg ringer tilbage senere.**	*yie ring•ah til•<u>ba</u>•yer <u>seh</u>•nah*
Bye.	**Farvel.**	*fah•<u>vehl</u>*
Where's the post office?	**Hvor ligger posthuset?**	*voar <u>li</u>•gah pohsd•hoo•serdh*
I'd like to send this to...	**Jeg vil gerne sende dette til...**	*yie vil <u>gehr</u>•ner <u>seh</u>•ner <u>deh</u>•der til...*

In Denmark, upon meeting, it is customary to shake hands for both men and women. Close friends (male-female/female-female) may give kiss one another on the cheeks. As a greeting, you could say **Går det godt?** (How's it going?) or **Hva så?** (What's up?). **Hej** is used both for hello or hi and bye.

De (the formal form of you) is generally no longer used to address strangers, but is restricted to formal letters, addressing the elderly or addressing members of the royal family. As a general rule, **du** can be used in all situations without offending anyone.

Can I…?	**Kan jeg…?** *kan yie…*	
access the internet here	**gå på internettet herfra** *gow paw in•tah•neh•derdh hehr• frah*	
check email	**tjekke min e-mail** *tjay•ker meen ee•mail*	
print	**printe** *prin•ter*	
plug in/charge my laptop/iPhone/iPad/BlackBerry?	**oplade min bærbare/iPhone/iPad/BlackBerry?** *ohb•la•der meen behr•barer/iPhone/iPad/BlackBerry*	
access Skype?	**bruge Skype?** *broo•er Skype*	
What is the WiFi password?	**Hvad er WiFi-passwordet?** *vadh her WiFi-pass•word•edh*	
Is the WiFi free?	**Er der gratis WiFi?** *ehr dehr ghra•tis WiFi*	
Do you have bluetooth?	**Har I bluetooth?** *hahr ee bluetooth?*	
Do you have a scanner?	**Har I en scanner?** *hah ee ehn scan•ner*	

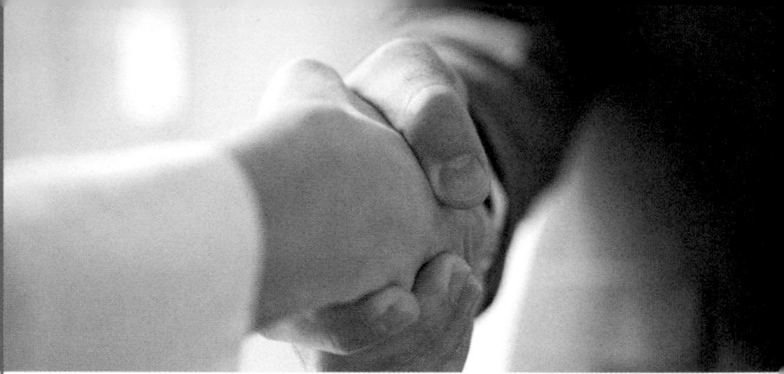

Social Media

Are you on Facebook/Twitter?	**Er du på Facebook/Twitter?** *her doo paw Facebook/Twitter*
What's your user name?	**Hvad er dit brugernavn?** *vadh ehr deet broo•er•nown*
I'll add you as a friend.	**Jeg vil tilføje dig som ven.** *yie vil til•foi•er die som vehn*
I'll follow you on Twitter.	**Jeg vil følge dig på Twitter.** *yie vil foil•ier die paw Twitter*
Are you following...?	**Følger du...?** *foil•ier doo*
I'll put the pictures on Facebook/Twitter.	**Jeg vil lægge billederne op på Facebook/Twitter.** *yie vil lay•ger bee•leh•ar op paw Facebook/Twitter*
I'll tag you in the pictures.	**Jeg vil tagge dig på billederne.** *yie vil tag•ge die paw bee•leh•arner*

Conversation

Hello!	**Hej!** *hie*
How are you?	**Hvordan har du det?** *Voar•dan har doo deh*
Fine, thanks.	**Godt, tak.** *goht tahk*
Excuse me!	**Undskyld!** *oan•skewl*

Do you speak English?	**Kan du tale engelsk?** *kan doo ta•ler ehng•erlsk*
What's your name?	**Hvad hedder du?** *vadh heh•dhah doo*
My name is…	**Mit navn er…** *meet nown ehr…*
Nice to meet you.	**Det glæder mig at træffe dig.** *deh glay•dhah mie ad treh•fer die*
Where are you from?	**Hvor kommer du fra?** *voar koh•mah doo frah*
I'm from the U.S./ the U.K.	**Jeg kommer fra USA/England.** *yie koh•mah frah oo•ehs•a/ehng•lan*
What do you do?	**Hvad laver du?** *vadh la•vah doo*
I work for…	**Jeg arbejder hos…** *yie ah•bey•dah hohs…*
I'm a student.	**Jeg studerer.** *yie stoo•deh•rah*
I'm retired.	**Jeg er pensionist.** *yie ehr pang•shoa•neest*

Romance

Would you like to go out for a drink/meal?	**Har du lyst til at gå ud og få en drink/ noget at spise?** *hah doo lurst til ad gow ood ow fow ehn drink/noa•erdh ad spee•ser*
What are your plans for tonight/tomorrow?	**Hvad er dine planer for i aften/i morgen?** *vadh ehr dee•ner pla•nah foh ee ahf•tern/ee mohn*
Can I have your number?	**Må jeg få dit nummer?** *mow yie fow deet noa•mah*
Can I join you?	**Må jeg komme med dig?** *mow yie koh•mer mehdh die*
Let me buy you a drink.	**Lad mig købe dig en drink.** *ladh mie kur•ber die ehn drink*
I love you.	**Jeg elsker dig.** *yie ehl-skah die*

Accepting & Rejecting

Thanks, I'd love to.	**Tak, det vil jeg meget gerne.** *tahk deh vil yie mie•erdh gehr•ner*
Where can we meet?	**Hvor skal vi mødes?** *voar skal vee mur•dhers*

I'll meet you at the bar/your hotel.	**Jeg møder dig i baren/på dit hotel.** *Yie mur•dhah die ee bahn/paw deet hoa•tehl*
I'll come by at…	**Jeg kommer klokken…** *yie koh•mah kloh•gehrn…*
Thank you, but I'm busy.	**Tak, men jeg er desværre optaget.** *tahk mehn yie ehr deh•svehr ohp•ta•erdh*
No thanks, I'm not interested.	**Nej tak, jeg er ikke interesseret.** *nie tahk yie ehr ig•ger in•trah•seh•erdh*
Leave me alone!	**Vær rar og lad mig være i fred!** *vehr rah ow la mie vay•er ee frehdh*
Stop bothering me!	**Lad mig være i fred!** *la mie vay•er ee frehdh*

Food & Drink

Eating Out

Can you recommend a good restaurant/bar?	**Kan du anbefale en god restaurant/bar?** *kan doo an·beh·fa·ler ehn goadh reh·stoa·rang/bah*
Is there a traditional Danish/an inexpensive restaurant nearby?	**Ligger der en typisk dansk/ikke så dyr restaurant i nærheden?** *li·gah dah ehn tew·peesk dansk/ig·ger saw dewr reh·stoa·rang ee nehr·heh·dhern*
A table for…, please.	**Et bord til…tak.** *eht boar til…tahk*
Can we sit…?	**Må vi sidde…?** *mow vee si·dher…*
here/there	**her/der** *hehr/dehr*
outside	**udenfor** *oo·dhern·foh*
at a non-smoking table	**ved et bord for ikke-rygere** *t vehdh ehboar foh ig·ger·rew·ah*
I'm waiting for someone.	**Jeg venter på nogen.** *yie vehn·dah paw noa·ern*
Where are the toilets?	**Hvor er toilettet?** *voar her toa·ee·leh·derdh*
I'd like a menu, please.	**Jeg vil gerne bede om et menukort, tak.** *yie vil gehr·ner beh ohm eht meh·new·kawd tahk*
What do you recommend?	**Hvad kan du anbefale?** *vadh kan doo an·beh·fa·ler*
I'd like…	**Jeg vil gerne have…** *yie vil gehr·ner ha…*
Some more, please.	**Jeg vil gerne have lidt mere, tak.** *yie vil gehr·ner ha lit meh·ah tahk*
Enjoy your meal.	**Velbekomme.** *vehl·beh·koh·mer*
Can I have the check [bill]?	**Kan jeg få regningen?** *kan yie fow rie·ning·ern*

Café Halvvejen

Is service included?	**Er drikkepenge inkluderet?**
	*ehr drig•ger•pehng•er in•kloo•**deh**•rerdh*
Can I pay by credit card?	**Kan jeg betale med kreditkort?**
	*kan yie beh•**ta**•ler mehdh kreh•deet•kawd*
Can I have a receipt?	**Kan jeg få en kvittering?**
	*kan yie fow ehn kvee•**teh**•ring*

Morgenmad (breakfast) is usually eaten quite early, since school and work often begin at 8:00 a.m. A typical breakfast includes buttered bread, **skæreost** (sliced cheese), creamy white cheese like **Havarti**, jam and coffee. **Frokost** (lunch) is often a simple meal of buttered bread and spreads. **Aftensmad** (dinner) begins at about 6:00 p.m. and is the main meal, as well as the only hot meal, of the day. Dinner may include several courses or may simply be a hearty soup followed by dessert.

Nyhavns caféen

Breakfast

bacon *bay·kohn*	bacon
brød *brurdh*	bread
smør *smur*	butter
koldt kødpålæg *kohlt kurdh·paw·laygh*	cold cuts
ost *oast*	cheese
blødkogt/hårdkogt æg	soft-/hard-boiled egg
blurdh·kohgd/h<u>aw</u>·kohgd ayg	
spejlæg *spiel·ayg*	fried eggs
røræg *rur·ayg*	scrambled eggs
syltetøj *sewl·der·toi*	jam
omelet *oa·mer·leht*	omelet
ristet brød *ris·terdh brurdh*	toast
pølser *purl·sah*	sausage
yoghurt *yoo·goord*	yogurt

YOU MAY SEE...

BEREGNING PER KUVERT	cover charge
DAGENS MENU	daily menu

Soup is, on many occasions, a meal on its own. If you'd like to try a traditional soup, order **aspargessuppe** (asparagus soup), **gule ærter** (split-pea soup), **frugtsuppe** (fruit soup) or chicken soup **med boller** (with meatballs).

Appetizers

leverpaté _leh·wah·pa·teh_	liver paté
(marineret/røget) makrel	(marinated/smoked)
(mah·ree·neh·rahdh/roi·erdh) ma·krehl	mackerel
muslinger _moos·ling·ah_	mussels
hummersuppe _hoa·mah·soa·per_	lobster chowder
klar suppe med boller og grønsager _klah_	vegetable soup
soa·per mehdh boh·lah ow grurn·sa·yah	with meatballs
hønsekødsuppe	chicken and vegetable soup
hurn·ser·kurdhs·soa·per	
salat _sa·lat_	salad

Meat

oksekød _ohk·ser·kurdh_	beef
kylling _kew·ling_	chicken
lam _lahm_	lamb
svinekød _svee·ner·kurdh_	pork

33

YOU MAY HEAR...

letstegt _leht·stehgt_	rare
medium _meh·dee·oam_	medium
gennemstegt _geh·nerm·stehgt_	well-done

| **ribbenssteg** *ree·behns·stie* | ribsteak |
| **kalvekød** *kal·ver·kurdh* | veal |

Fish & Seafood

torsk *tohsk*	cod
sild *seel*	herring
hummer *hoa·mah*	lobster
laks *lahks*	salmon
rejer *rie·ah*	shrimp [prawns]

Vegetables

bønner *bur·nah*	beans
kål *kowl*	cabbage
gulerødder *goo·ler·rur·dhah*	carrots

Smørrebrød (open-faced sandwiches), comprised of buttered rye bread and sliced meat or cheese, have been a part of Danish cuisine for a long time; however, the fancier, more elaborate **smørrebrød** eaten on festive occasions appeared only in the late 1800s. Today **smørrebrød** is topped with a variety of delicacies: mounds of shrimp, eel, smoked salmon, marinated or smoked herring, liver paste, roast beef or pork and steak tartare. The sandwich is then garnished with a number of other ingredients such as: raw onions, cress, scrambled eggs, egg yolk, radishes, chives and pickled cucumbers.

Many large restaurants serve **smørrebrød**. You can select a traditional combination such as **dyrlægens natmad** (liver paté, corned beef and aspic **smørrebrød**), **rullepølse** (spiced meat roll) or **stjerneskud** (fish and shrimp **smørrebrød**), or you can name the individual items that you prefer.

champienoner	mushrooms
shahm·peen·yong·ah	
løg *loi*	onions
ærter *ehr·dah*	peas
kartofler *ka·tohf·lah*	potatoes
tomater *toa·m**a**·dah*	tomatoes

Sauces & Condiments

salt *salt*	salt
peber *pe·wer*	pepper
sennep *seh·nerp*	mustard
ketchup *ket·youp*	ketchup

In Denmark, **moms** (sales tax or value-added tax) and service charges are included in your bill in hotels and restaurants, in admissions charges and purchase prices as well as taxi fares. Tips may be given for outstanding service, but they are not necessary.

Fruit & Dessert

æble _ay·bler_	apple
banan _ba·nan_	banana
citron _see·troan_	lemon
appelsin _ah·berl·seen_	orange
pære _pay·rah_	pear
jordbær _yoar·behr_	strawberries
is _ees_	ice cream
chokolade/vanilje	chocolate/vanilla
shoa·koa·la·dher/va·nil·yer	
kage _ka·yer_	cake
fromage _froa·ma·sher_	mousse
karamelrand _kah·rah·mehl·rehn_	caramel custard

Akvavit is a very popular drink in Denmark. Like vodka, it's distilled from potatoes, though barley is also used. The color varies according to the herbs and spices with which the drink is flavored. Often served with a beer chaser, **akvavit** is drunk ice-cold, and makes an ideal accompaniment to Danish appetizers.

A favorite Danish pastime is visiting pubs, though you can also find wine bars and cocktail bars. A traditional pub is called a **bodega** (beer bar). There you'll see Danes enjoying the local brews and playing dice. Dice can be requested at the bar.

Another option is to check out the many **hyggelige** cafes. Cafes range from those where you can order a drink and a simple sandwich to those with sophisticated decor and jet-set clientele.

If you're in the mood for music, there are plenty of dance clubs as well as regular live music shows to be found.

Drinks

May I see the wine list/drink menu?	**Må jeg se vinlisten/listen med drinks?** *mow yie seh veen•lis•tern/lis•tern mehdh drinks*
What do you recommend?	**Hvad kan du anbefale?** *vadh kan doo an•bch•fa•ler*
I'd like a bottle/glass of red/white wine.	**Jeg vil gerne bede om en flaske/et glas rødvin/hvidvin.** *yie vil gehr•ner beh ohm ehn flas•ger/eht glas rurdh•veen/veedh•veen*
The house wine, please.	**Hustes vin, tak.** *hoo•sets veen tahk*
Another bottle/glass, please.	**En flaske/Et glas mere, tak.** *ehn flas•ger/eht glas meh•ah tahk*
I'd like a local beer.	**Jeg vil gerne bede om en lokal øl.** *yie vil gehr•ner beh ohm ehn loa•kal url*
Let me buy you a drink.	**Lad mig byde dig på en drink.** *ladh mie bew•dher die paw ehn drink*
Cheers!	**Skål!** *skowl*
A coffee/tea, please.	**En kop kaffe/te, tak.** *ehnkohpkah•fer/teh tahk*
Black.	**Sort.** *soart*

With milk.	**Med mælk.** *mehdh mehlk*
With sugar.	**Med sukker.** *mehdh soa·gah*
With artificial sweetener.	**Med sødemiddel.** *mehdh sur·dher·mee·dherl*
. . . please.	**. . . tak.** *. . . tahk*
juice	**Juice** *djoos*
soda	**Sodavand** *soa·da·van*
sparkling/ still water	**Danskvand/Kildevand** *dansk·van/kee·ler·van*

If you're not in the mood for Danish beer, there are a number of other drinks to enjoy. Strong filtered coffee is enjoyed throughout the day, even with meals. If you prefer tea, herbal tea is popular. **Varm chokolade** (hot chocolate) is often served to children, but is also enjoyed by adults. For a unique drink, try **hyldeblomstsaft** (elderflower juice), which is a delicacy that has made a comeback. Water will be labeled as **danskvand** or **mineralvand** (sparking or mineral water).

Leisure Time

Sightseeing

Where's the tourist information office?	**Hvor ligger turistinformationen?** *Voar li·gah too·reest·in·foh·ma·shoa·nern*
What are the main points of interest?	**Hvad er de vigtigste seværdigheder?** *Vadh ehr dee vig·tee·ster seh·vehr·dee·heh·dhah*
Do you offer tours in English?	**Tilbyder I turer på engelsk?** *til·bew·dhah ee too·ah paw ehng·erlsk*
Can I have a map/ guide?	**Må jeg få et kort/en guidebog?** *mow yie fow eht kawd/ehn guide·bow*

Shopping

Where is the market/ mall [shopping centre]?	**Hvor ligger markedet/butikscentret?** *voar li·gah mah·ker·dherd/boo·teeks·sehn·tahdh*

YOU MAY SEE...

ÅBEN/LUKKET	open/closed
INDGANG/UDGANG	entrance/exit

I'm just looking.   **Jeg ser mig bare omkring.**
                         yie sehr mie bah ohm•kring

Can you help me?   **Kan du hjælpe mig?**
                         kan doo yehl•per mie

I'm being helped.   **Jeg får hjælp.** *yie faw yehlp*

How much?   **Hvor meget koster det?** *voar mie•erdh*
                         kohs•dah deh

Denmark is known for its modern design and quality craftsmanship around the world. You can peruse the fine silver and jewelry pieces at the **Georg Jensen** shops in Copenhagen and Århus. **Bang & Olufsen**, known internationally for its excellent audiovisual equipment, has shops throughout the country. **Ecco** shoes are easy to find and **Lego** is available in all toy and department stores. **Holmegård Glas, Stelton, Royal Copenhagen** and other well-known Danish designs can be purchased from interior design shops as well as department stores. Though your suitcase might not be big enough, Danes are also famous for their mid-century and modern furniture.

Moms (sales tax or value-added tax) and service charges are already included in your final bill in restaurants. Tips for outstanding service are a matter of personal choice.

I'd like...	**Jeg vil gerne have...** *yie vil gehr·ner ha...*
That's all, thanks.	**Det var det hele, tak.** *deh vah deh heh·ler tahk*
Where do I pay?	**Hvor kan jeg betale?** *voar kan yie beh·ta·ler*
I'll pay in cash/ by credit card.	**Jeg vil gerne betale kontant/med kreditkort.** *yie vil gehr·ner beh·ta·ler kohn·tant/ mehdh kreh·deet·kawd*
Can I have a receipt?	**Kan jeg få en kvittering?** *kan yie fow ehn kvee·teh·ring*

Sport & Leisure

When's the game?	**Hvornår starter kampen?** *voar·naw stah·dah kahm·bern*
Where's...?	**Hvor er...?** *voar ehr...*
the beach	**stranden** *strah·nern*

Denmark is an excellent country for shopping. Even in the capital, most shopping can be done on foot. Many of the major international retail stores are located in **Strøget** and **Købmagergade**, Copenhagen's main pedestrian streets. You can also check out **Vesterbro**, the western part of **Istegade** and the area around **Enghaveplads**. There, you'll find lots of trendy boutiques and pleasant cafes.

For everything under one roof, visit the **Magasin du Nord**, Scandinavia's largest department store, or the shopping malls: **Field's, Fisketorvet, Frederiksberg Centret** or **Illum.**

Regular store hours are Monday to Friday from 9:00 a.m. to 5:30 p.m. On Friday stores are open until as late as 8:00 p.m. and Saturday they are generally open from 10:00 a.m. to 4:00 or 5:00 p.m. Most stores are closed on Sunday.

The mild climate and topography of Denmark are not particularly good for winter sports. However, ice hockey and ice skating are popular.

the park	**parken** _pah_•gern
the pool	**svømmebassinet** _svur_•mer•ba•sehng•erdh
Is it safe to swim/ dive here?	**Er det sikkert at svømme/dykke her?** _ehr deh sig•gahd ad svur•mer/dur•ker hehr_
Can I hire golf clubs?	**Kan jeg leje golfkøller?** _kan yie lie•er gohlf•kur•lah_
How much per hour?	**Hvad koster det per time?** _vadh kohs•dah deh pehr tee•mer_
How far is it to…?	**Hvor langt er der til…?** _voar lahngt ehr dehr til…_
Can you show me on the map?	**Kan du vise mig det på kortet?** _kan doo vee•ser mie deh paw kaw•derdh_

Going Out

What is there to do in the evenings?	**Hvad laver man her om aftenen?** *Vadh la·vah man hehr ohm af·tern*
Do you have a program of events?	**Har du et program over arrangementerne?** *hah doo eht proa·grahm ow·ah ah·rahng·sheh·mang·ah·ner*
What's playing at the movies [cinema] tonight?	**Hvad går der i biografen i aften?** *vadh gaw dehr ee bee·oa·gra·fern ee af·tern*
Where's...?	**Hvor er...?** *voar ehr...*
the downtown area	**den indre by** *dehn in·drah bew*
the bar	**baren** *bah·ern*
the dance club	**diskoteket** *dees·koa·teh·kerdh*
Is this area safe at night?	**Er dette område sikkert om natten?** *ehr deh·ter ohm·row·dhe sig·gard ohm na·dern*

Baby Essentials

Do you have...?	**Har du...?** *har doo...*
a baby bottle	**en suttefl aske** *ehn soo·der·flas·ker*

baby food	**babymad** *bay·bew·madh*
baby wipes	**nogen vådservietter** *noa·ern voadh·sehr·vee·eh·dah*
a car seat	**et barnesæde** *eht bah·ner·say·dher*
a children's menu	**en børnemenu** *ehn bur·ner·meh·new*
a children's portion	**en børneportioner** *bur·ner·poh·shoa·nah*
a child's seat/ highchair	**et barnesæde/en høj stol** *eht bah·ner·say·dher/ehn hoi stoal*
a crib	**en barneseng** *ehn bah·ner·sehng*
diapers [nappies]	**nogen bleer** *noa·ern bleh·ah*
formula	**noget mælkeerstatning** *noa·erdh mehl·ker·ehr·stad·ning*
a pacifier [dummy]	**en sut** *ehn soot*
a playpen	**en kravlegård** *ehn krow·ler·gaw*
a stroller [pushchair]	**en klapvogn** *ehn klahp·vown*
Can I breastfeed the baby here?	**Må jeg amme babyen her?** *mow yie ah·mer bay·bee·ern hehr*
Where can I change the baby?	**Hvor kan jeg skifte babyen?** *voar kan yie skeef·der bay·bee·ern*

Disabled Travelers

Is there…?	**Er der…?** *ehr dehr…*
access for the disabled	**adgang for handicappede** *adh·gahng for han·dee·kahp·per·dher*
a wheelchair ramp	**en rampe til kørestole** *ehn rahm·ber til kur·ah·stoa·ler*
a disabled-accessible toilet	**et handicaptoilet** *eht han·dee·kahp·toa·ee·lehd*
I need…	**Jeg har brug for…** *yie hah broo foh…*
assistance	**hjælp** *yehlp*
an elevator [lift]	**en elevator** *ehn eh·ler·va·toh*
a ground-floor room	**et værelse i stueetagen** *eht vehrl·ser ee stoo·er·eh·ta·shern*
Speak louder/more slowly, please.	**Vær rar og tal lidt højere/lidt langsommere.** *vehr rah ow ta·ler lit hoi·ah/lit lang·sohm·ah*

Health & Emergencies

Emergencies

Help!	**Hjælp!** *yehlp*
Go away!	**Gå væk!** *gow vehk*
Stop thief!	**Stop tyven!** *stohp tew·vern*
Get a doctor!	**Tilkald læge!** *til·kal lay·er*
Fire!	**Det brænder!** *deh brahn·nah*
I'm lost.	**Jeg er faret vild** *yie ehr fah·erdh veel*
Can you help me?	**Kan du hjælpe mig?** *kan doo yehl·per mie*
Call the police!	**Ring til politiet!** *ring til poa·lee·tee·erdh*
Where's the police station?	**Hvor ligger politistationen?** *voar li·gah poa·lee·tee·sta·shoa·nern*
My child is missing.	**Mit barn er blevet væk.** *meet bahn ehr bleh·erdh vehk*

YOU MAY HEAR...

Udfyld venligst denne formular.
oodh·fewl vehn·leest deh·neh foh·moo·lah
Fill out this form.

Vis venligst dit ID.
Vees vehn·leesd deet ee deh
Your ID, please.

Hvornår/Hvor skete det?
voar·naw/voar skeh·der deh
When/Where did it happen?

Hvordan ser han/hun ud?
voar·dan sehr han hoon oodh
What does he/she look like?

Health

I'm sick [ill].	**Jeg er syg.** *yie ehr sew*
I need an English-speaking doctor.	**Jeg har brug for en læge, der taler engelsk.** *yie hah broo foh ehn lay·er dehr ta·lah ehng·erlsk*
It hurts here.	**Det gør ondt her.** *deh gur ohnt hehr*
Where's the nearest pharmacy?	**Hvor er det nærmeste apotek?** *voar ehr deh nehr·meh·ster ah·poa·tehk*
I'm (...months) pregnant.	**Jeg er (...måneder) henne.** *yie ehr (...maw·nedh·ar) heh·ner*
I'm on...	**Jeg tager...** *yie tah...*
I'm allergic to antibiotics/penicillin.	**Jeg er allergisk over for antibiotika/pencilin.** *yie ehr a·lehr·geesk ow·ah·foh an·tee·bee·oa·tee·ka/pehn·see·leen*

In an emergency, dial **112**.

Dictionary

A

a (with common nouns) en; **(with neuter nouns)** et
able kunne
about cirka
acetaminophen [paracetamol] en æske paracetamol
adapter adapter
ambulance ambulance
American amerikaner
and og
antiseptic cream antiseptisk creme
Australia Australien

B

baby baby
baby bottle sutteflaske
baby food babymad
baby wipes vådservietter
babysitter babysitter
back ryg
backache rygsmerter
backpack rygsæk
bad dårlig
bag (purse) taske; **(shopping)** pose
Band-Aid [plaster/bandage] plaster
beige beige
bikini bikini
bird fugl
black sort
bland (food) har ingen smag

blue blå
bottle opener oplukker
bowl skål
boy dreng
boyfriend kæreste
bra bh
British (person) brite; *adj* britisk
brown brun

C

cabin (ship) kahyt
cafe café
camera kamera
can opener dåseåbner
castle slot; borg
cigarette cigaret
cold (illness) forkølelse; *adj* kold
comb kam
condom kondom
contact lens solution noget kontaküinsevæske
corkscrew proptrækker
cup kop

D

dairy mejeri
damaged beskadiget
dance club diskotek
dance *n* dans; *v* danse
danger fare
dangerous farlig
Danish (person) dansker; *adj* dansk
deodorant deodorant

dlabetic diabetiker
dog hund
doll dukke

E

each hver
ear øre
ear drops øredråber
earache ondt i ørerne
early tidligt
earring ørenring

F

fabric (cloth) stof
face ansigt
facial ansigtsbehandling
factory fabrik
fair messe
fall v falde
family familie
fan ventilator
fork gaffel

G

gallery galleri
game spil
garage garage
garbage skrald
garden have
gas benzin
gasoline benzin
girl pige

girlfriend kæreste
glass (drinking) glas
good god
gray grå
great (excellent) storartet
green grøn

H

hair hår
hair dryer hårtørrer
hairbrush hårbørste
haircut klipning
hairdresser frisør
hairspray hårlak
hand hånd
hand cream håndcreme
hot (temperature) varm
husband mand

I

I jeg
ice is
icy (weather) iskoldt
identification (card) id-kort
if hvis
ill [BE] syg
illness sygdom
important vigtig
imported importeret
impressive imponerende
in i
include iberegne

Indoor indendørs
injection indsprøjtning
I'd like... Jeg vil gerne have...
insect repellent insekt-spray
Irish (person) irlænder, *adj* irsk

J

jacket jakke
jaw kæbe
jeans cowboybukser

K

keep beholde
kerosene petroleum
key nøgle
key card nøglekort
kiddie pool børnebassin
kidney nyre
kind *adj* rar; *n* slags
kiss *v* kysse
knee knæ
knife kniv
knitwear strikvarer
know vide

L

label etiket
lace blonde
lactose intolerant laktoseintolerant
lake sø
lamp lampe
large stor
lighter lighter

lotion lotion
love *v* elske

M

magazine blad
magnificent storartet
maid stuepige
mail *n* post; *v* poste
mailbox postkasse
make-up *n* sminke
mall butikscenter
matches tændstikker
medium medium
museum museum

N

nail (body) negl
nail clippers negleklipper
nail file neglefil
nail salon neglesalon
name navn
napkin serviet
nappy [BE] ble
narrow smal
nationality nationalitet
natural naturlig
nausea kvalme
napkin serviet
nurse sygeplejerske

O

o'clock klokken
occupation stilling

occupied optaget
office kontor
off-licence [BE] vinhandel
oil spiseolie
old gammel
old town gamle bydel
on på
on time til tiden
once en gang
or eller
orange (color) orange

P

pacifier (baby's) sut
packet pakke
pad (sanitary) hygiejnebind
pail spand
pain smerte
painkiller smertestillende middel
paint n maling; v male
park n park; v parkere
pen pen; kuglepen
pink lyserød
plate tallerken
purple violet

R

race væddeløb
race track væddeløbsbane
racket (sport) ketsjer
radio radio
railway station [BE] jernbanestation

rain regnvejr
raincoat regnfrakke
rape *n* voldtægt
razor barbermaskine
razor blade barberblad
red rød

S

safe n **(vault)** boks; **(not in danger)** sikker
safety pin sikkerhedsnål
sailboat sejlbåd
sale *n* salg; **(bargains)** udsalg
same samme
salty saltet
sauna sauna
sand sand
sandal sandal
sanitary napkin hygiejnebind
scissors saks
shampoo shampoo
sharp (pain) skarp
shave *n* barbering
shaving brush barberbørste
shoe sko
small lille
sneaker gummisko
snow sne
soap sæbe
sock sok
spicy krydret
spoon ske

stamp *n* **(postage)** frimærke; *v* **(ticket)** stemple
suitcase kuffert
sun sol
sunglasses solbriller
sun-tan lotion solcreme
sweater sweater
sweatshirt sweatshirt
swimming trunks badebukser

T

table bord
tampon tampon
terrible frygtelig
tie slips
tissue papirslommetørklæde
toilet paper toiletpapir
toothbrush tandbørste
toothpaste tandpasta
touch *v* røre
tour tur
tourist office turistkontor
tow truck kranbil
towards mod
towel håndklæde
town by
town hall rådhus
tough sejt
toy legetøj
toy store legetøjsforretning
traffic light trafiklys
T-shirt T-shirt

U

ugly grim
umbrella paraply; **(beach)** parasol
unconscious bevidstløs
under under
underground station [BE] metrostation
underpants underbukser

V

vacancy ledigt værelse
vacant ledig
vacation ferie
vaccinate vaccinere
vegan veganer
vegetarian vegetar

W

wait *v* vente
waiter/waitress tjener; kvindelig tjener
wake-up call morgenvækning
walk *n* gåtur
wallet tegnebog
warm (temperature) varm; *v* **(reheat)** opvarme
wash vaske
washing machine vaskemaskine
watch *n* ur
water vand
weather forecast vejrudsigt
week uge
weekend weekend
well godt
what hvad

wheel hjul
wheelchair kørestol
when hvornår
where hvor
which hvilken
white hvid
with med
wife kone
without uden

Y

year år
yellow gul
yes ja
yesterday i går
yet endnu
young ung
youth hostel vandrehjem

Z

zoo zoologisk have

Swedish

Essentials

Hello!	**Hej!** *hay*
Goodbye.	**Hej då.** *hay·doa*
Yes.	**Ja.** *yah*
No.	**Nej.** *nay*
Okay.	**Okej.** *oa·kay*
Excuse me! (to get attention)	**Ursäkta!** *eur·shehk·ta*
Excuse me. (to get past)	**Ursäkta mig.** *eur·shehk·ta may*
I'm sorry.	**Jag är ledsen.** *yahg air led·sehn*
I'd like...	**Jag skulle vilja ha...** *yahg skuh·ler vihl·ya hah...*
How much does it cost?	**Hur mycket kostar det?** *heur mew·ker* *kos tar dee*
And/Or	**Och/Eller** *ock/ehl·lehr*
Please	**Tack.** *tak*
Thank you.	**Tack.** *tak*
You're welcome.	**Ingen orsak.** *ihn·gen ohr·sak*
Where is...?	**Var ligger...?** *vahr lih·gehr...*
I'm going to...	**Jag ska resa till...** *yahg skah ree·sa tihl...*
My name is...	**Jag heter...** *yahg hee·tehr...*
Can you speak more slowly?	**Kan du tala lite långsammare?** *kan deu tah·la lee·teh loang·sahm·a·rer*
Can you repeat that?	**Kan du upprepa det?** *kan deu uhp ree·pa dee*
I don't understand.	**Jag förstår inte.** *yahg furr·stoar in·ter*
Do you speak English?	**Talar du engelska?** *tah·lar deu ehng·ehl·ska*

I don't speak Swedish. **Jag talar inte svenska.**
yahg <u>tah</u>•lar <u>ihn</u>•ter <u>svehns</u>•ka

Where is the **Var är toaletten?**
restroom [toilet]? *vahr air to**a**•ah•<u>leh</u>•ten*

Help! **Hjälp!** *yehlp*

Numbers

0	**noll**	*nohl*
1	**ett**	*eht*
2	**två**	*tvo**a***
3	**tre**	*tree*
4	**fyra**	*<u>few</u>•ra*
5	**fem**	*fehm*
6	**sex**	*sehx*
7	**sju**	*sheu*
8	**åtta**	*oh•<u>ta</u>*
9	**nio**	*<u>nee</u>•oa*
10	**tio**	*<u>tee</u>•oa*
11	**elva**	*<u>ehl</u>•va*
12	**tolv**	*tohlv*
13	**tretton**	*<u>treh</u>•tohn*

You'll find the pronunciation of the Swedish letters and
words written in gray after each sentence to guide you. Simply
pronounce these as if they were English, noting that any underlines
and bolds indicate an additional emphasis or stress or a lengthening of
a vowel sound. As you hear the language being spoken, you will quickly
become accustomed to the local pronunciation and dialect.

14	**fjorton** _fyeur_·tohn
15	**femton** _fehm_·tohn
16	**sexton** _sehx_·tohn
17	**sjutton** _sheu_·tohn
18	**arton** _ar_·tohn
19	**nitton** _nih_·tohn
20	**tjugo** _shcheu_·yoa
21	**tjugoett** _shcheu_·goa·eht
22	**tjugotvå** _shcheu_·goa·tv**oa**
30	**trettio** _treh_·tee·oa
31	**trettioett** _treh_·tee·oa·eht
40	**fyrtio** _fuhr_·tee·oa
50	**femtio** _fehm_·tee·oa
60	**sextio** _sehx_·tee·oa
70	**sjuttio** _sheu_·tee·oa
80	**åttio** _oh_·tee·oa
90	**nittio** _nih_·tee·oa
100	**hundra** _huhn_·dra
101	**hundraett** _huhn_·dra·eht
200	**två hundra** _tv**oa**_ huhn·dra
500	**fem hundra** _fehm_ huhn·dra

63

1,000	**ett tusen** *eht teu·sehn*
10,000	**tio tusen** *tee·oa teu·sehn*
1,000,000	**en miljon** *ehn mihl·yoan*

Time

What time is it?	**Hur mycket är klockan?**
	heur mew·ker air kloh·kan
It's noon [midday].	**Klockan är tolv.** *kloh·kan air tolv*
It's twenty after [past] four.	**Den är tjugo över fyra.**
	dehn air shcheu·goa ur·ver few·ra
It's a quarter to nine.	**Den är kvart i nio.** *dehn air kvart ee nee·oa*

Sweden officially follows the 24-hour clock. Formal communication, such as public transporation schedules and TV programming, follows this system. However, in ordinary conversation, time is generally expressed as shown above, often with the addition of **på morgonen** (in the morning), **på förmiddagen** (mid-morning), **på eftermiddagen** (in the afternoon), **på kvällen** (in the evening) and **på natten** (at night).

Sweden follows a day-month-year format instead of the month-day-year format used in the U.S.
E.g.: July 25, 2008; **25/07/08** = 7/25/2008 in the U.S.

5:30 a.m.	**Halv sex på morgonen.**	
	halv sehx p**oa** _mor_•oh•nehn	
5:30 p.m.	**Halv sex på kvällen.**	
	halv sehx p**oa** _kveh_•lehn	

Days

Monday	**måndag** _moan_•dahg
Tuesday	**tisdag** _tees_•dahg
Wednesday	**onsdag** _oans_•dahg
Thursday	**torsdag** _toash_•dahg
Friday	**fredag** _free_•dahg
Saturday	**lördag** _lurr_•dahg
Sunday	**söndag** _surn_•dahg

Dates

yesterday	**igår** ee•_goar_
today	**idag** ee•_dahg_
tomorrow	**imorgon** ee•mo•ron
day	**dag** dahg
week	**vecka** _veh_•ka
month	**månad** _moa_•nad
year	**år** oar
Happy New Year!	**Gott Nytt År!** got nyet oar
Happy Birthday!	**Grattis på födelsedagen!**
	grah•tis p**oa** furd•el•seh•dahg•ehn

The two most important holidays in Sweden are Midsummer and Christmas. **Midsommardagen** (Midsummer) is celebrated with midsummer poles (similar to the maypole) and traditional songs and dances. Traditional food includes **matjesill** (pickled herring), fresh fish and schnapps. For **Juldagen** (Christmas), special cakes and other delicious treats are prepared, such as **pepparkakor** (ginger cookies), **saffranbullar** (saffron buns) and **julbord** (Christmas **smörgåsbord,** a festive buffet). Though not an official holiday, **Luciadagen** (St. Lucia Day) on December 13 marks the beginning of the Christmas season. Swedes also celebrate the beginning of spring on April 30, which is known as **Valborgsmässoafton,** with huge bonfires, fireworks and singing. June 6 is **Flaggans dag** (Flag Day), the national day of Sweden. Streets are decorated with yellow and blue, the colors of the Swedish flag, patriotic speeches are made and traditional games and meals are enjoyed.

Months

January	**januari** *ya•neu•ah•ree*
February	**februari** *fehb•reu•ah•ree*
March	**mars** *mash*
April	**april** *ap•rihl*
May	**maj** *maiy*
June	**juni** *yeu•nee*
July	**juli** *yeu•lee*
August	**augusti** *a•guhss•tee*
September	**september** *sehp•tehm•behr*
October	**oktober** *ohk•toa•behr*
November	**november** *noh•vehm•behr*
December	**december** *dee•sehm•behr*

Arrival & Departure

I'm here on vacation [holiday]/business.	**Jag är här på semester/affärsresa.** *Yahg air hair poa seh•mehs•ter/a•fairs•ree•sa*
I'm going to...	**Jag ska resa till...** *yahg skah ree•sa tihl...*
I'm staying at a hotel/youth hostel.	**Jag bor på hotell/vandrarhem.** *yahg boar poa hoh•tehl/vahnd•rar•hehm*

Money

Where's...?	**Var ligger...?** *vahr lih•gehr...*
the ATM	**bankomaten** *bank•oa•mah•tehn*
the bank	**banken** *bank•ehn*

YOU MAY SEE...

Sweden's monetary unit is the **krona** (singular) or **kronor** (plural) abbreviated to **SEK**.
The **krona** is divided into **öre**.
Coins: 50 **öre**, 1 **krona**, 5 and 10 **kronor**
Banknotes: 20, 50, 100, 500 and 1000 **kronor**

Cash can be obtained from a **Bankomat** (ATM) with MasterCard, Visa, Eurocard, American Express and other international credit cards or with a debit card.

Banks will often refer customers with traveler's checks to the nearest **växelkontor** (currency exchange) such as Forex or X-Change. The latter are often located near or in points of departure/arrival such as airports and train stations, but can also be found in city centers. Remember to bring your passport with you for identification when you want to exchange money or cash traveler's checks.

Most banks close at 3:00 p.m. daily, though some offer late opening one day a week, often on Thursdays.

the currency exchange office	**växelkontoret** _vehx•ehl•kohn•**toar**•eht_
What time does the bank open/close?	**När öppnar/stänger banken?** _nair urp•nahr/stehng•ehr bank•ehn_
I'd like to change dollars/pounds into kronor.	**Jag skulle vilja växla dollar/pund till kronor.** _yahg skuh•ler vihl•ya vehx•la doh•lar/pund tihl kroa•nohr_
I want to cash some traveler's checks [cheques].	**Jag skulle vilja lösa in några resecheckar.** _yahg skuh•ler vihl•ya lur•sa ihn noa•gra ree•seh•sheh•kar_
Can I pay in cash?	**kan jag betalar kontant?** _kan yahg beh•tah•la kohn•tant_
Can I pay by credit card?	**Kan jag betala med kreditkort?** _kan yahg beh•tah•la meed kreh•deet•koart_

For Numbers, see page 62.

Getting Around

How do I get to town?	**Hur kommer jag till staden?**
	heur koh•mehr yahg tihl stahd•ehn
Where is…?	**Var ligger…?** *vahr lih•gehr…*
the airport	**flygplatsen** *flewg•plats•ehn*
the train [railway] station	**järnvägsstationen** *yairn•vehgs•sta•shoa•nehn*
the bus station	**bussterminalen** *bus•tehr•mee•nah•lehn*

The subway in Stockholm is efficient and easy to use. It runs from 5:00 a.m. to midnight on weekdays. Tickets are valid for one hour from the time they are stamped and can be bought from ticket booths; discount cards can be purchased from **Pressbyrån** (a newsstand). Tickets can also be purchased at **SL Centers**, some tourist offices and certain grocery stores. The public transportation websites will have information on these retailers and businesses and what types of tickets they sell. Day and multi-day cards are also available. Subway and bus tickets in Stockholm are interchangeable.

Regular boat and ferry services, carrying cars and passengers, link Sweden to neighboring countries such as Norway, Denmark and Germany as well as to the U.K. Ferry services from Stockholm to the vacation destinations of **Åland** and **Gotland** in the Baltic Sea are very popular, as are ferries to Finland, Estonia and Latvia. Not to be missed are the ferry and steamer trips from Stockholm to the many surrounding islands, known as **Skärgården** (the Archipelago).

the subway [underground] station	**tunnelbanestationen** _teu·nehl·bah·neh·sta·shoan·ehn_
How far is it?	**Hur långt är det?** _heur loangt air dee_
Where can I buy tickets?	**Var kan jag köpa biljetter?** _vahr kan yahg chur·pa bil·yeht·tehr_
A one-way [single]/ round-trip [return].	**Enkel./Retur.** _ehng·kehl/reh·teur_
How much does it cost?	**Hur mycket kostar det?** _heur mew·ker kos·tar dee_

Which gate?	**Vid vilken gate?**
	veed vihl•kehn gayt
Which line?	**Vilken kö?** *vihl•kehn kur*
Which platform?	**Vilken plattform?**
	vihl•kehn plat•fohrm
Where can I get a taxi?	**Var kan jag få tag på en taxi?**
	vahr kan yahg foa tahg poa ehn tax•ee
Please take me to this address.	**Var snäll och kör mig till denna address.**
	vahr snehl ohk churr may tihl deh•na ad•rehs
To...Airport, please.	**Till...Flygplats, tack.**
	tihl...flewg•plats tak
I'm in a rush.	**Jag har bråttom.**
	yahg hahr broa•tohm
I'd like a map.	**Jag skulle vilja ha en karta.** *Yahg skuh•ler vihl•ya hah ehn kahr•ta*

Public transportation in Sweden is an excellent and well-maintained system that includes **bussar** (buses), **tunnelbanan** (subways), **spårvagnar** (trams) and **tåg** (trains). All of these run frequently, usually between 5:00 a.m. and midnight on weekdays and a bit later on weekends. Most cities and towns have a bus system, though only a few have trams and subways. While it is possible to purchase single tickets for the different modes of public transportation, it is more cost efficient to purchase a card or set of tickets if you are going to be using a particular network frequently. Most major cities have websites that provide up-to-date information on routes, tickets and prices; many of the sites have English as a language option.

Taxis can be found at stands marked **Taxi.** You can also flag
down a taxi in the street, especially near hotels and bus and
train stations. Calling a taxi by phone is a third option; numbers are
available from your concierge or a local phone book. The sign **Ledig**
(free), when lit, indicates that the taxi is available.

Tickets

When is...to	**När går...till Uppsala?**
	nair goar...tihl uhp·sah·la Uppsala?
the (first) bus	**(första) bussen** *(furs·ta) buhs·ehn*
the (next) flight	**(nästa) flyg** *(nehs·ta) flewg*
the (last) train	**(sista) tåget** *(sihs·ta) toa·geht*
One ticket/Two	**En biljett/Två biljetter, tack.** *ehn bil·yet/tvoa*
tickets, please.	*bil·yeht·er tak*
For today/tomorrow.	**Till dagens/imorgon.**
	tihl dah·gens/ee·mo·ron
...ticket.	**...biljett.** *...bihl·yeht*
A one-way [single]	**En enkel** *ehn ehng·kehl*
A return-trip	**En retur** *ehn reh·teur*
A first class	**En första klass** *ehn furr·sta klas*
I have an e-ticket.	**Jag har en e-biljett.** *yahg hahr ehn ee·bihl·yet*
How long is the trip?	**Hur lång tid tar resan?**
	heur loang teed tahr ree·san
Is it a direct train?	**Är det ett direkttåg?**
	air deh·ta eht dihr·ekt·toag
Could you tell me	**Kan du tala om för mig när jag ska stiga av?**
when to get off?	*kan deu tah·la ohm furr may nair yahg skah stee·ga afv*

Statens järnvägar or **SJ** (the Swedish State Railway) operates an extensive network covering the entire country, while also offering international connections to Oslo, Copenhagen and Berlin. The X2000 train, which reaches speeds up to 200 km/h, serves many of Sweden's greater cities and towns. Long-distance trains have restaurant cars and/or buffets, and there are also sleepers and couchettes for both first and second class. The system is reliable and comfortable, and offers a wide range of travel options with respect to schedule and cost. Discount tickets are available for young children, families, students and senior citizens. Special travel cards and programs are also available. On some trains, marked **R** or **IC**, you must reserve a seat by purchasing a **sittplatsbiljett** in addition to your travel ticket. For extraordinary scenery, try the northern **Inlandsbanan** (Inland Railway) service, which runs from Mora in Dalarna to Gällivare beyond the Arctic circle. The **Vildmarksexpressen** (Wilderness Express) has old 1930s coaches and a gourmet restaurant, and runs on the same line between Östersund and Gällivare, with stops and excursions.

YOU MAY HEAR...

rakt fram *rahkt fram*	straight ahead
till vänster *tihl <u>vehn</u>·stehr*	on/to the left
till höger *tihl <u>hur</u>·gehr*	on/to the right
i/runt hörnan *ee/ruhnt <u>hur</u>·nan*	on/around the corner
mitt emot *miht ee·<u>moat</u>*	opposite
bakom *<u>bah</u>·kohm*	behind
bredvid *<u>breh</u>·veed*	next to
efter *<u>ehf</u>·tehr*	after
norr/söder *nohr/<u>sur</u>·dehr*	north/south
öster/väster *<u>urs</u>·tehr/<u>vehs</u>·tehr*	east/west
vid trafikljusen *veed tra·<u>feek</u>·y<u>eu</u>s·ehn*	at the traffic light
vid avfarten *veed <u>afv</u>·far·tehn*	at the exit

I'd like to…my reservation.	**Jag skulle vilja…min bokning.** *Yahg <u>skuh</u>•ler <u>vihl</u>•ya…mihn <u>boak</u>•nihng*
cancel	**avbeställa** *<u>afv</u>•beh•steh•la*
change	**ändra** *<u>ehn</u>•dra*
confirm	**bekräfta** *beh•<u>krehf</u>•ta*

For Time, see page 64.

Car Hire

Where can I hire a car?	**Var kan jag hyra en bil?** *vahr kan yahg <u>hew</u>•ra ehn beel*
I'd like to hire…	**Jag skulle vilja hyra…** *yahg <u>skuh</u>•ler <u>vihl</u>•ya <u>hew</u>•ra…*
a cheap/small car	**en billig/liten bil** *en bihl•eeg/lee•tehn beel*
an automatic/ manual car	**en bil med automatväxel/manuell** *ehn beel meed ah•toa•<u>maht</u>•vehx•ehl/mah•nuh•ehl*
a car with air-conditioning	**en bil med luftkonditionering** *ehn beel meed <u>luhft</u>•kohn•dee•shoa•<u>neer</u>•ihng*
a car seat	**en bilbarnstol** *ehn beel•<u>barn</u>•stoal*

How much does it cost…?	**Hur mycket kostar det…?** *heur <u>mew</u>•ker <u>kos</u>•tar d**ee**…*
per day/week	**per dag/vecka** *pair dahg/<u>veh</u>•ka*
Are there any special weekend rates?	**Har ni särskilda helgrabatter?** *hahr nee <u>sair</u>•shihl•da <u>hely</u>•ra•bat•ehr*

Street parking, parking lots and, in some cases, parking garages will be available in most of Sweden's cities and larger towns. Street parking is generally metered in city centers and downtown areas. A blue circular sign with a red slash tells you where parking is prohibited. There will be signs indicating whether or not parking is free. In places where parking is metered, a ticket allowing you to park for a specific period of time will need to be purchased. If this is the case, tickets can be purchased from a **biljettautomat** (ticket machine). You pay for the amount of time you want to park and then place the ticket on the dashboard in plain sight. In some cases, parking may be free. In this instance, there will be signs posted with time limits, usually up to two or three hours.

If you are looking for something comfortable and reasonably priced, **Svenska Turistföreningen** or **STF** (the Swedish Tourist Club) is an excellent place to start. Here you can search for accommodations such as **vandrarhem** (youth hostels). If you are a member of **STF** or Hostelling International you get a member discount. Generally, room options include dormitory style rooms, male-only and female-only rooms, as well as smaller private rooms or family rooms. You are usually expected to bring your own towels and sheets as these are usually not provided, but can be rented. Shared kitchen facilities are often available, so that you can buy food at the local supermarket and prepare your own meals. Some hostels offer breakfast.

Places to Stay

Can you recommend a hotel in…?	**Kan du rekommendera ett hotel i…?** *kan deu reh·koh·mehn·dee·ra eht hoh·tehl ee…*
I have a reservation.	**Jag har bokat rum.** *yahg hahr boa·kat ruhm*
My name is…	**Jag heter…** *yahg hee·tehr…*

Do you have a room…?	**Har ni ett ledigt rum…?** *hahr nee eht lee·dihgt ruhm…*
for one/two	**för en person/två personer** *furr ehn pehr·shoan/tvoa pehr·shoan·ehr*
with a bathroom	**med badrum** *meed bahd·ruhm*

There is a wide range of places to stay in Sweden, from luxury to budget. Budget options include **privatrum** (private rooms), much like bed and breakfasts, or **stugor** (cabins) and **lägenheter** (apartments). Cabins and apartments are usually rented out on a weekly basis, but one- or two-night stays may also be an option. Information can be found at the local tourist office; you may also see signs along the road indicating that there is a vacancy in a cabin nearby. Motorists can look for **motel** (motels); these are reasonably priced with restaurants and car-friendly facilities. When looking for somewhere to stay in university towns such as Stockholm, Göteborg or Lund, staying at a **sommarhotel** (summer hotel) can be a good choice. Student dormitories are open to tourists in the summer and are a good option if you are traveling in a group. Families can enjoy a **familjehotell** (a family hotel), which has special rates for groups sharing the same room (three to six beds). These only operate during the summer months. All-inclusive accommodation is also available in the form of a **turisthotell** (tourist hotel) or **pensionat** (boarding house). These are clean and comfortable hotels or guesthouses that are often found at summer resorts and winter sport areas. Sweden also offers first class and deluxe hotels, usually found in larger cities and towns. Prices and amenities vary but the standards are usually high. Breakfast is usually included. When booking somewhere to stay during the summer months and high tourist season it is important to book in advance.

with air-conditioning	**med luftkonditionering** *meed luhft·kohn·dee·shoa·neer·ihng*
For tonight.	**För ikväll.** *furr ee·kvehl*
For two nights.	**För två nätter.** *furr tvoa neh·tehr*
For one week.	**För en vecka.** *furr ehn veh·ka*
How much?	**Hur mycket kostar det?** *heur mew·ker kos·tar dee*
Do you have anything cheaper?	**Har ni någonting billigare?** *hahr nee noa·gohn·tihng bihl·ee·ga·rer*
When's check-out?	**När måste vi checka ut?** *nair mos·ter vee sheh·ka eut*
Can I leave this in the safe?	**Kan jag lämna detta i kassaskåpet?** *Kan yahg lehm·na deh·ta ee ka·sah·skoa·peht*
Could we leave our baggage here until…?	**Kan vi lämna vårt bagage här till klockan…?** *kan vee lehm·na voart ba·goash hair tihl kloh·kan…*
Could I have the bill/receipt, please?	**Kan jag få räkningen/kvittot, tack?** *Kan yahg foa rairk·nihng·en/kvih·toht tak*
I'll pay in cash/by credit card.	**Jag betalar kontant/med kreditkort.** *Yahg beh·tah·lar kohn·tant/meed kreh·deet·koart*

79

Communications

Where's an internet cafe?	**Var finns det ett internetkafé?** *vahr fihns dee eht ihn·tehr·neht·ka·feh*
Can I access the internet/check email here?	**Kan jag komma ut på internet/kola e-post här?** *kan yahg koh·ma eut poa ihn·tehr·neht/koa·la ee·pohst hair*
How much per hour/ half hour?	**Hur mycket kostar det per timme/halvtimme?** *heur mew·ker kos·tar dee pair tihm·er/halv·tihm·er*
How do I connect/ log on?	**Hur loggar jag in?** *heur loh·gar yag ihn*
Can I have a phone card?	**Kan jag få ett telefonkort?** *kan yahg foa eht teh·leh·foan·koart*
Can I have your phone number?	**Kan jag få ditt telefonnummer?** *kan yahg foa diht teh·leh·foan·nuhm·ehr*
Here's my number/ email address.	**Här är mitt nummer/min e-postadress.** *hair air miht nuhm·ehr/mihn ee·pohst·ad·rehs*
Call me.	**Var snäll och ring mig.** *vahr snehl ohk ring may*
Please text me.	**Var snäll och skicka ett sms till mig.** *Vahr snehl ohk shih·ka eht ehs·ehm·ehs tihl may*

I'll text you.	**Jag skickar ett sms till dig.**
	yahg shih•kar eht ehs•ehm•ehs tihl day
Email me.	**Skicka en e-post till mig.**
	shih•ka ehn ee•pohst tihl may
Hello. This is…	**Hej. Det här är…** *hay dee hair air…*
I'd like to speak to…	**Jag skulle vilja tala med…** *yahg skuh•ler*
	vihl•ya tah•la meed…
Repeat that, please.	**Kan du upprepa det, tack.**
	kan deu uhp•ree•pa dee tak
I'll be in touch.	**Jag hör av mig snart.**
	yahg hur afv may snahrt
Goodbye.	**Hej då.** *hay doa*
Where is the post office?	**Var ligger posten?** *vahr lih•gehr pohs•tehn*
I'd like to send this to…	**Jag skulle vilja skicka det här till…**
	yahg skuh•ler vihl•ya shih•ka dee hair tihl…
Can I…?	**Kan jag…?** *kahn yahg…*
access the internet	**gå ut på internet**
	goa eut poa ihn•tehr•neth
check my email	**kolla min e-post**
	kohla meen eh•pohst

plug in/charge my laptop/iPhone/iPad/BlackBerry?	**sätta i/ladda min laptop/iPhone/iPad/BlackBerry?** *sehta ih/ladha meen laptop/iPad/BlackBerry*
access Skype?	**använda Skype?** *an·vehn·a Skype*
What is the WiFi password?	**Vilket är WiFi-lösenordet?** *vihl·keht wai·fai-lur·sehn·oarde*
Is the WiFi free?	**Är WiFi:n gratis?** *air wai·fain grah·tihs*
Do you have bluetooth?	**Har ni blåtand?** *hahr nee bloa·tand*
Do you have a scanner?	**Har ni en skanner?** *Hahr nee ehn ska·nehr*

Social Media

Are you on Facebook/Twitter?	**Finns du på Facebook/Twitter?** *Fihns deu poa Facebook/Twitter*
What's your user name?	**Vilket användarnamn har du?** *Vihl·keht an·vehn·dar·namn hahr deu*
I'll add you as a friend.	**Jag lägger till dig som vän.** *yahg lehg·ehr tihl day sohm vehn*
I'll follow you on Twitter.	**Jag följer dig på Twitter.** *Yahg fuhl·yehr day poa Twitter*

Are you following…?	**Följer du…?** *Fuhl·yehr deu…*
I'll put the pictures on Facebook/Twitter.	**Jag lägger ut bilderna på Facebook/Twitter.** *yahg lehg·ehr eut bihl·dehr·na poa Facebook/Twitter*
I'll tag you in the pictures.	**Jag taggar bilderna.** *yahg ta·gar bihl·dehr·na*

Conversation

Hello!	**Hej!** *hay*
How are you?	**Hur står det till?** *heur stoar dee tihl*
Fine, thanks. And you?	**Bra, tack. Och du?** *brah tak ohk deu*
Excuse me!	**Ursäkta!** *eur·shehk·ta*
Do you speak English?	**Talar du engelska?** *tah·lar deu ehng·ehl·ska*
What's your name?	**Vad heter du?** *vahd hee·tehr deu*
My name is…	**Jag heter…** *yahg hee·tehr…*
Nice to meet you.	**Trevligt att träffas.** *treev·lihgt at trehf·as.*
Where are you from?	**Var kommer du ifrån?** *vahr ko·mehr deu ee·froan*
I'm from the U.S./U.K.	**Jag kommer från USA/Storbritannien.** *yahg koh·mehr froan eu ehs ah/stoap·bree·tan·yehn*
What do you do?	**Vad sysslar du med?** *vahd sews·lar deu meed*
I work for…	**Jag jobbar på.** *yahg yohb·ar poa…*

| I'm a student. | **Jag är student.** *yahg air <u>stuh</u>•dent* |
| I'm retired. | **Jag är pensionär.** *yahg air pang•shoa•<u>nair</u>* |

Romance

Would you like to go out for a drink/dinner?	**Har du lust att ta en drink/gå ut och äta?** *hahr deu luhst at tah ehn drihnk/g**oa** eut ohk <u>air</u>•ta*
What are your plans for tonight/tomorrow?	**Vad har du för planer för ikväll/imorgon?** *vahd hahr deu furr <u>plah</u>•nehr furr ee•<u>kvehl</u>/ee•<u>mo</u>•ron*
Can I have your number?	**Kan jag få ditt telefonnummer?** *kan yahg f**oa** diht teh•leh•<u>**foa**n</u>•nuhm•ehr*

Swedes shake hands when greeting someone and when saying goodbye; this applies for meeting new people but is also often the case with colleagues or acquaintances. When you meet someone for the first time, shake hands and give your name. As in many countries, titles are more commonly used by the older generation, but you will sometimes hear **herr** (Mr.), **fru** (Mrs.) and **fröken** (Miss) used, as well as professional titles, e.g., **doktor** (doctor), **ingenjör** (engineer), etc.

May I join you?	**Får jag göra dig sällskap?** *foar yahg yurra dihg sehl•skahp*
Can I buy you a drink?	**Får jag bjuda på en drink?** *foar yahg byeu•da poa ehn drihnk*
I love you.	**Jag älskar dig.** *yahg ehl•skar day*

Accepting & Rejecting

Thank you. I'd love to.	**Tack, det vill jag gärna.** *tak dee vihl yahg yair•na*
Where should we meet?	**Var ska vi träffas?** *vahr skah vee treh•fas*
I'll meet you at the bar/your hotel.	**Vi träffas i baren/på ditt hotell.** *vee treh•fas ee bahr•en/poa diht hoh•tehl*
I'll come by at...	**Jag kommer...** *yahg koh•mehr...*
Thank you, but I'm busy.	**Tack, men jag är upptagen.** *tak men yahg air uhp•tah•gehn*
I'm not interested.	**Jag är inte intresserad.** *yahg air in•ter in•treh•see•rad*
Leave me alone, please!	**Kan du lämna mig ifred, tack!** *kan deu lehm•na may ee•freed tak*
Stop bothering me!	**Sluta störa mig!** *sluh•ta stur•ra may*

85

Food & Drink

Eating Out

Can you recommend a good restaurant/bar?	**Kan du rekommendera en bra restaurang/pub?** *kan deu reh•koh•mehn•**dee**•ra ehn brah rehs•teu•rang/peub*
Is there a traditional Swedish/an inexpensive restaurant nearby?	**Finns det något värdshus/någon billigare restaurang i närheten?** *fihns dee noa•goht vairds•heus/noa•gohn bihl•ih•ga•rer rehs•teu•rang ee nair•hee•tehn*
A table for..., please.	**Ett bord för..., tack.** *eht bohrd furr...tak*
Could we sit...?	**Får vi sitta...?** *foar vee siht•a...*
here/there	**här/där** *hair/dair*
outside	**ute** *eu•ter*
in a non-smoking area	**vid bord för icke-rökare** *veed bohrd furr ee•keh•rur•ka•rer*
I'm waiting for someone.	**Jag väntar på någon.** *yahg vairn•tar poa noa•gohn*
Where are the toilets?	**Var finns toaletten?** *vahr fihns toa•ah•leh•tehn*
A menu, please.	**En meny, tack.** *ehn meh•neu tak*

86

What do you recommend?	**Vad rekommenderar du?**
	*vahd reh•koh•mehn•**dee**•rar deu*
I'd like...	**Jag skulle vilja ha...** *yahg <u>skuh</u>•ler <u>vihl</u>•ya hah...*

If you've never heard of typical Swedish food, you may at least
be familiar with the famous **smörgåsbord** — it is a buffet meal
on a grand scale, presented on a large, beautifully decorated table.
You start at one end of the table, usually the one with the cold seafood
dishes, marinated herring, **Janssons frestelse** (literally, Jansson's
temptation, a potato and anchovies casserole) and salad. Then you
work your way through the cold meat, meatballs, sausage, omelets and
vegetables. Finally, you end at the cheeseboard and desserts. You're
welcome to start all over again; the price is set, and you can eat as much
as you like. You will find that the Swedes tend to drink **akvavit** (aquavit)
or beer with the feast, although an accompanying glass of wine is
becoming more common for those who find **akvavit** too strong.
At Christmas time, the **smörgåsbord** becomes a **julbord** (Christmas
buffet), popular in homes and restaurants alike.

Some more…, please.	**Lite mer…, tack.** _lee_·ter meer…tak
Enjoy your meal.	**Smaklig måltid.** _smahk_·lihg _moal_·teed
The check [bill], please.	**Kan jag få räkningen, tack.** kan yahg foa _rairk_·nihng·ehn tak
Is service included?	**Är serveringsavgiften inräknad?** air ser·_veeh_·rihngs·afv·_yihf_·tehn _ihn_·rairk·nad

Frukost (breakfast) is usually served from 7:00 to 10:00 a.m. Hotels and guesthouses offer a large buffet selection of cheese, cold meat, bread, eggs, cereals and **filmjölk** (thick yogurt). **Lunch** (lunch) is served from as early as 11:00 a.m. Although many Swedes have a warm meal at lunchtime, some opt for a sandwich or a salad. This is the best time to try the **dagens rätt** (specialty of the day). **Middag** (dinner) is normally eaten early, around 6:00 or 7:00 p.m., though many restaurants continue serving until late, especially at the weekend. Many Swedes will also eat a meal later in the evening, referred to as **kvällsmål;** this evening meal usually includes sandwiches, yogurt or soup.

When it comes to eating out, there are many options, ranging from fast-food stands to five-star restaurants. If you are looking for a quick bite to eat, then a **gatukök** (fast-food stand) is an easy choice. If you are looking for more traditional cuisine, this can be found at a **värdshus** (roadside restaurant), **kafé** (cafe) or **restaurang** (restaurant).

Can I pay by credit card?	**Kan jag betala med kreditkort?** *kan yahg beh·tah·la meed kreh·deet·koart*
Can I have the receipt, please?	**Kan jag få kvittot, tack?** *kan yahg foa kvih·toht tak*

Breakfast

bacon *bay·kohn*	bacon
bröd *brurd*	bread
smör *smur*	butter
kallskuret *kal·skeu·reht*	cold cuts [charcuterie]
ägg *ehg*	egg
kokt ägg *koakt ehg*	boiled egg
stekt ägg *steekt ehg*	fried egg
äggröra *ehg·rur·ra*	scrambled eggs
sylt *sewlt*	jam
omelett *ohm·eh·leht*	omelet
rostat bröd *roahs·tat brurd*	toast
korv *kohrv*	sausage
yoghurt *yoh·geurt*	yogurt

Appetizers

färska räkor <u>fairs</u>·ka <u>rair</u>·kohr	unshelled shrimp [prawns]
fisksoppa fihsk·<u>sop</u>·a	fish soup
gravlax <u>grafv</u>·lax	marinated salmon
grönsakssoppa <u>grurn</u>·<u>sahks</u>·<u>sohp</u>·a	vegetable soup
kycklingsoppa <u>chewk</u>·lihng·<u>sohp</u>·a	chicken soup
löjrom <u>lury</u>·rohm	bleak roe with raw onions and and sour cream; served on toast
sallad <u>sal</u>·ad	salad
sillbricka <u>sihl</u>·brih·ka	variety of marinated herring
S.O.S. (smör, ost och sill) ehs oa ehs (sm**ur** oast ohk sil)	a small plate of marinated herring, bread, butter and cheese

Although Sweden still has many small, specialty shops, they are slowly giving way to **köpcentrum** (shopping centers), especially in larger towns. You can still find markets that sell fresh fruit and vegetables as well as flowers and some handicrafts. **Julmarknaden** (the traditional Christmas market) in Stockholm is reminiscent of times gone by. Supermarkets can be found in most large towns, cities and suburbs. **Närbutiker** (corner shops), as well as **Pressbyrån** (newsstand chain) sell a good range of food. In Stockholm, **Östermalmshallen** and **Hötorgshallen** (market halls) sell fresh meat — including reindeer and moose — fish and poultry. Swedes enjoy a variety of fish and seafood, and one will find a good selection in most restaurants and supermarkets. If you visit Sweden in August, you will no doubt enjoy a **kräftkalas** (crayfish party). There is not much meat on a crayfish, but when helped down with a few glasses of **akvavit** (aquavit) and some salad and cheese, it makes for an unforgettable evening.

YOU MAY HEAR...

blodig _bloa·dihg_	rare
medium _mee·dee·uhm_	medium
genomstekt _ye·nom·steekt_	well done

toast skagen _toast skah·gehn_	toast with chopped shrimp [prawns] in mayonnaise, topped with bleak roe
tomatsoppa _toa·maht·soh·pa_	tomato soup
viltpastej _vihlt·pa·stay_	game pâté

Meat

biffkött _bihf·churt_	beef
kyckling _chewk·lihng_	chicken
lamm _lamm_	lamb
fläsk _flehsk_	pork
biffstek _bihf·steek_	steak
kalvkött _kalv·churt_	veal

Fish & Seafood

torsk *tohrshk*	cod
sill *sihl*	herring
sillbricka <u>*sihl*</u>·*brih*·*ka*	variety of marinated herring
sillsallad <u>*sihl*</u>·*sal*·*ad*	beet and herring salad
hummer <u>*huhm*</u>·*ehr*	lobster
lax *lax*	salmon
räkor <u>*rair*</u>·*kohr*	shrimp [prawns]

A service charge as well as **moms** (sales tax) is included in hotel and restaurant bills, but you are expected to round up a restaurant bill to the nearest **krona**. Tipping is generally not expected, but it's always appreciated if the service has been exceptionally good. It is customary to give a small tip to hairdressers, barbers, taxi drivers and porters.

For afternoon tea (usually enjoyed with lemon) or coffee you can do no better than the typical Swedish **konditori** (patisserie or coffee shop). Help yourself to as many cups as you like while indulging in a slice of **prinsesstårta** (sponge cake with cream and custard, covered with green marzipan), **mazarin** (almond tart, topped with icing) or a **wienerbröd** (Danish pastry). Try **saffransbullar** (saffron buns) and **pepparkakor** (ginger cookies) at Christmas. Most **konditori** are self-service, but some of the more elegant ones and those in hotels provide full service. Coffee is definitely the national drink, and it is always freshly brewed. It is commonly drunk black, but ask for **mjölk** (milk) or **grädde** (cream) if you like it that way.

Vegetables

böna... *bur·na...*	...bean
bond *boand*	broad
bryt <u>*brewt*</u>	kidney
grön *grurn*	green
vax <u>*vax*</u>	butter

YOU MAY SEE...

KUVERTAVGIFT	cover charge
FAST PRIS	fixed-price
MENY	menu
DAGENS MENY	menu of the day
DRICKS (INTE) INRÄKNAD	service (not) included
SPECIALITETER	specials

kål *koal*	cabbage
morot *moa·roht*	carrot
champinjon *sham·pihn·yoan*	mushroom
lök *lurk*	onion
ärta *air·ta*	peas
potatis *poa·tah·tihs*	potato
tomat *toa·maht*	tomato

Sauces & Condiments

peppar *peh·par*	pepper
salt *salt*	salt
senap *see·nap*	mustard
ketchup *keht·shuhp*	ketchup

Fruit & Dessert

äpple *ehp·leh*	apple
banan *ba·nahn*	banana
citron *see·troan*	lemon
apelsin *a·pehl·seen*	orange
päron *pai·rohn*	pear
jordgubbe *yoard·guh·ber*	strawberry
glass *glas*	ice cream
choklad *shoa·klahd*	chocolate
vanilj *va·nihly*	vanilla
kaka *kah·ka*	cake
äppelpaj *eh·pehl·pay*	apple tart
vaniljsås *va·nihly·soas*	vanilla sauce, often like custard
grädde *greh·der*	cream

Drinks

May I see the wine list/drink menu?	**Kan jag få se vinlistan/drinklistan?** *kan yahg foa see veen·lihs·tan/drihnk·lihs·tan*
What do you recommend?	**Vad rekommenderar ni?** *vahd reh·koh·mehn·dee·rar nee*
I'd like a bottle/glass of red/white wine.	**Jag skulle vilja ha en flaska/ett glas rött/vitt vin.** *yahg skuh·ler vihl·ya hah ehn flas·ka/eht glahs ruhrt/viht veen*
The house wine, please.	**Husets vin, tack.** *heu·sehts veen tak*
Another bottle/glass, please.	**En flaska/Ett glas till, tack.** *ehn flas·ka/eht glahs tihl tak*
I'd like a local beer.	**Jag skulle vilja ha en öl från trakten.** *yahg skuh·ler vihl·ya hah ehn url fron trak·tehn*
Let me buy you a drink.	**Får jag bjuda på en drink.** *foar yahg byeu·da poa ehn drihnk*
Cheers!	**Skål!** *skoal*
A coffee/tea, please.	**En kopp kaffe/te, tack.** *ehn kohp ka·fer/tee tak*
Black.	**Svart.** *Svart*
With...	**Med...** *meed...*
milk	**mjölk** *myuhlk*

95

Food & Drink

sugar	**socker**	_soh_•kehr
artificial sweetener	**sötningsmedel**	_surt_•nihngs•_mee_•dehl
decaf	**utan koffein**	eu•tan koh•_feen_
…, please.	**…, tack.**	…tak
Juice	**Juice**	yoas
Soda [soft drink]	**sodavatten**	
		soa•da•va•tehrn
Sparkling water	**Vatten med kolsyra**	
		_va_•tehrn meed _koal_•**sew**•ra
Still water	**Vatten utan kolsyra**	
		_va_•tehrn _eu_•tan _koal_•**sew**•ra

96

Beer is probably the most popular alcoholic drink in Sweden, and there are many good Swedish breweries. Beer with an alcohol content above 3%, called **starköl**, can only be bought in **Systembolaget** (state liquor stores); **lättöl** and **folköl**, which are below 3% alcohol content, can be bought in grocery stores and supermarkets. You will find many well known international beers, but the most common are Carlsberg, Heineken and Swedish brews such as Pripps and Falcon.

Leisure Time

Sightseeing

Where's the tourist information office?	**Var ligger turistinformationen?** *vahr lih•gehr teu•rihst•ihn•fohr•ma•shoan•ehn*
What are the main points of interest?	**Vad finns det för sevärdheter?** *vahd fihns dee furr see•vaird•hee•tehr*
Do you have tours in English?	**Finns det några turer på engelska?** *fihns dee noa•gra teu•rehr poa ehng•ehl•ska*
Can I have a map/ guide, please?	**Kan jag få en karta/guide, tack?** *kan yahg foa ehn kahr•ta/gujd tak*

Shopping

Where is the market/ mall [shopping centre]?	**Var ligger orget/affärscentrumet?** *vahr lih•gehr tohr•yeht/a•ffairs•sehn•truhm•eht*
I'm just looking.	**Jag tittar bara.** *yahg tih•tar bah•ra*
Can you help me?	**Kan du hjälpa mig?** *kan deu yehlp•a may*
I'm being helped.	**Jag får hjälp, tack.** *yahg foar yehlp tak*
How much does it cost?	**Hur mycket kostar det?** *heur mew•ker kos•tar det*

YOU MAY SEE...

ÖPPET/STÄNGT	open/closed
INGÅNG/UTGÅNG	entrance/exit

When it comes to souvenirs, whether you are looking for something traditional or modern, you are sure to find just the thing in Sweden. **Träslöjd** (woodwork), **hemslöjd** (handicrafts), **keramik** (ceramics) and Swedish crystal are popular, traditional souvenirs. The **dalahäst** (Dala horse) is perhaps one of the most famous and ubiquitous souvenirs; traditionally, its color is a reddish-orange, but the horses can now be found in a wide range of colors and sizes. Sweden is known for its design, which is evident in its selection of **porslin** (fine china) and ceramics. Some well-known manufacturers include **Höganäs Keramik** and **Rörstrand**, the latter being the second oldest porcelain manufacturer in Europe, founded in 1746. Sweden is also famous for its glass and crystal, with respect to both design and quality. **Glasriket** (the kingdom of glass) located in Småland, in southeastern Sweden, has around 15 glass factories, including some of the most famous glassworks in Sweden, such as **Kosta Boda**, **Orrefors** and **Nybro**. Factory tours are often available. In addition to the traditional Swedish handicrafts mentioned above, **sameslöjd** (**Sámi** handicraft) is something that should not be overlooked. The **Sámi** are known for their beautiful crafts, which include jewelry and knives carved from reindeer antlers, jewelry made from beaded pewter and reindeer leather as well as a wide range of clothing in reindeer leather and different types of fur.

This/That one, thanks.	**Den här/där, tack.** *dehn hair/dair tak*
I'd like…	**Jag skulle vilja ha…**
	yahg skuh•ler vihl•ya hah…
That's all, thanks.	**Det var allt, tack.** *dee vahr alt tak*

Although Sweden still has many small, specialty shops,
Köpcentrum (malls) are becoming more and more common,
especially in larger towns. Many chain and department stores, such
as **Åhléns** and **Kappahl** and **Hennes & Mauritz**, have branches all
over the country, all of which sell quality goods. In the well-established
Stockholm department store **NK**, you can find almost anything,
though it can be quite expensive. Designer goods can be found at
DesignTorget in Stockholm. For traditional handicrafts look for signs
with **hemslöjd** (handicraft); in Stockholm, these can be found at
Svensk Hemslöjd and **Svenskt Hantverk** (traditional handicraft
stores). Many towns have colorful markets, where you can buy
anything from fresh fruit and vegetables to flowers and handicrafts.
Julmarknaden (Christmas market) in Stockholm in the Old Town and
Skansen (outdoor park and museum), are historic shopping areas.

Where do I pay?	**Var kan jag betala?** *vahr kan yahg beh·tah·la*
I'll pay in cash/by credit card.	**Jag vill betala kontant/med kreditkort.** *yahg vihl beh·tah·la kohn·tant/meed kreh·deet·koart*
A receipt, please.	**Kvittot, tack.** *kvih·tot tak*

Sports and recreation are popular, and there are excellent sports facilities everywhere, ranging from **golf** (golf), **fiske** (fishing), **tennis** (tennis) and **fotboll** (soccer) to **skidåkning** (skiing) and **ishockey** (ice hockey). Tourist offices should have contact information for the various sports facilities in your area. Swedes also love the great outdoors, and the country has much to offer when it comes to **bergklättring** (mountain climbing), **vandring** (hiking), **ridsport** (horsebackriding), **cykelåkning** (cycling), **paddla kanot** (canoeing) and **segling** (boating). Whether you are looking for a day hike or planning a longer trip, some great choices include **Kebnekaise**, which is Sweden's highest mountain, **Kungsleden**, **Bohusleden** or **Padjelantleden**. There are a lot of options for cyclists, both amateurs and professionals, and popular cycle routes include **Kustlinjen** and **Sverigeleden**.

Sport & Leisure

When's the game?	**När börjar matchen?** *nair <u>bur</u>•yar <u>ma</u>•shchehn*
Where's...?	**Var ligger...?** *vahr <u>lih</u>•gehr...*
the beach	**stranden** <u>stran</u>•dehn
the park	**parken** <u>park</u>•ehn
the pool	**simbassängen** <u>slhm</u>•ba•sehng•ehn
Is it safe to swim/ dive here?	**Kan man simma/dyka här utan risk?** *kan man <u>sihmm</u>•a/<u>dew</u>•ka hair <u>eu</u>•tan rihsk*
Can I rent [hire] golf clubs?	**Kan man hyra golfklubbor?** *kan man <u>hew</u>•ra <u>gohlf</u>•kluh•bohr*
How much per hour?	**Vad kostar det per timme?** *vahd <u>kos</u>•tar dee pair <u>tihm</u>•er*
How far is it to...?	**Hur långt är det till...?** *heur <u>loangt</u> air dee tihl...*
Can you show me on the map?	**Kan du visa mig på kartan?** *kan deu <u>vee</u> sa may poa <u>kahr</u>•tan*

Going Out

What's there to do at night?	**Vad kan man göra på kvällarna?** *vahd kan man <u>yur</u>•ra p**oa** <u>kvehl</u>•ar•na*
Do you have a program[me] of events?	**Har ni ett evenemangsprogram?** *hahr nee eht eh•vehn•eh•<u>mangs</u>•proa•gram*
What's playing at the movies [cinema] tonight?	**Vad visas på bio ikväll?** *vahd <u>vee</u>•sas p**oa** <u>bee</u>•oa ee•<u>kvehl</u>*
Where's…?	**Var ligger…?** *vahr <u>lih</u>•gehr…*
the downtown area	**centrum** *<u>sehn</u>•truhm*
the bar	**baren** *<u>bah</u>•rehn*
the dance club	**diskoteket** *dis•koh•<u>tee</u>•keht*
Is this area safe at night?	**Är detta område säkert på natten?** *ehr deh•ta ohm•roh•deh seh•kehrt poh na•tehn*

Baby Essentials

Do you have…?	**Har ni…?** *hahr nee…*	
a baby bottle	**en nappflaska** *ehn nap·flas·ka*	
baby food	**babymat** *behy·bih·maht*	
baby wipes	**våtservetter för barn** *voat·ser·veht·er furrbahrn*	
a car seat	**en bilbarnstol** *ehn beel·bahrn·stoal*	
a children's menu	**en barnmeny** *ehn bahrn·meh·new*	
a children's portion	**en barnportion** *bahrn·pohrt·shoan*	
a highchair	**en barnstol** *ehn bahrn·stoal*	
a crib	**en barnsäng** *ehn bahrn·sehng*	
diapers [nappies]	**blöjor** *blury·ohr*	
formula	**välling** *vehl·ihng*	
a pacifier [dummy]	**en napp** *ehn nap*	
a playpen	**ett lekrum** *eht leek·ruhm*	
a stroller [pushchair]	**en sittvagn** *ehn siht·vangn*	
Can I breastfeed the baby here?	**Får jag amma barnet här?** *foar yahg ah·ma bahr·neht hair*	
Where can I change the baby?	**Var kan jag byta på babyn?** *vahr kan yahg bew·ta poa bai·been*	

For Food & Drink, see page 86.

103

Disabled Travelers

Is there…?	**Finns det…?** *fihns det…*
access for the disabled	**ingång för rörelsehindrade** *in•goang furr rur•rehl•seh•hihn•dra•der*
a wheelchair ramp	**en rullstolsramp** *ehn reul•stoals•ramp*
a handicapped-[disabled-] accessible toilet	**en handikappanpassad toalett** *ehn hand•ee•kap•an•pas•ad toa•ah•leht*
I need…	**Jag behöver…** *yahg beh•hur•ver…*
assistance	**hjälp** *yehlp*
an elevator [lift]	**en hiss** *ehn hihs*
a ground floor room	**ett rum på bottenvåningen** *eht ruhm poa boh•tehrn•voa•nihng•hen*
Speak louder/more slowly.	**Var snäll och tala högre/långsammare.** *vahr snehl ohk tah•la hur•greh/loang•sam•a•rer*

Health & Emergencies

Emergencies

Help!	**Hjälp!** *yelp*
Go away!	**Ge er iväg!** *yeh ehr ee·vairg*
Stop thief!	**Stoppa tjuven!** *stop·a shcheu·vehn*
Get a doctor!	**Hämta en läkare!** *hehm·ta ehn lair·ka·rer*

YOU MAY HEAR...

Fyll i blanketten, tack. *fewl ee blan·keht·ehn tak*	Please fill out this form.
Er legitimation, tack. *ehr lehg·ee·tih·ma·shoan tak*	Your identification, please.
När/Var hände det? *nair/vahr hehn·dehr dee*	When/Where did it happen?
Hur ser han/hon ut? *hewr seer han/hoan eut*	What does he/she look like?

Fire!	**Det brinner!** *dee brihn•ehr*
I'm lost.	**Jag har gått vilse.** *yahg hahr goat vihl•ser*
Can you help me?	**Kan du hjälpa mig?** *kan deu yehl•pa may*
Call the police!	**Ring polisen!** *rihng poa•lee•sehn*
Where's the nearest police station?	**Var ligger närmaste polisstation?** *vahr lih•gehr nair•mas•ter poo•lees•sta•shoan*
My child is missing.	**Mitt barn har kommit bort.** *miht bahrn hahr koh•miht bohrt*

Health

I'm sick [ill].	**Jag är sjuk.** *yahg air sheuk*
I need an English-speaking doctor.	**Jag behöver en engelsktalande läkare.** *yahg beh•hur•vehr ehn ehng•ehlsk•tahl•an•der lair•ka•rer*
It hurts here.	**Det gör ont här.** *dee yurr oant hair*
Where's the nearest pharmacy?	**Var är närmaste apotek?** *vahr air nair•mas•teh a•poa•teek*
I'm (...months) pregnant.	**Jag är (...månader) gravid.** *Yahg air (...moh•na•dehr) gra•veed*
I'm taking...	**Jag tar... (medicin).** *yahg tahr...*
I'm allergic to antibiotics/penicillin.	**Jag är allergisk mot antibiotika/penicillin.** *yahg air a•lehr•gihsk moat an•tih•bee•oa•tee•ka/ pehn•eh•si•leen*

The emergency number in Sweden is **112**.

Dictionary

A

about (approximately) omkring
accept *v* acceptera
accident olycka
accommodation logi
acetaminophen paracetamol
across över
acupuncture akupunktur
adapter adapter
address *n* adress
and och
antiseptic cream antiseptisk salva
aspirin huvudvärkstablett

B

baby baby
baby bottle nappflaska
baby formula välling
baby wipes våtservetter för barn
babysitter barnvakt
backpack ryggsäck
bad dålig
bag (shopping) påse
baggage cart bagagekärra
baggage claim bagageutlämning
bakery bageri
band (music group) band
bandage (gauze) gasbinda
bank bank
bank charge bankavgift

banknote sedel
bar bar
barber herrfrisör
battlefield slagfält
beige beige
bikini bikini
black svart
bland smaklöst
blue blått
bottle opener flasköppnare
bowl djup tallrik
boy pojke
boyfriend pojkvän
bra behå
brown brun

C

cabin stuga
cafe kafé
calender kalender
call v **(phone)** ringa
calm lugn
camera kamera
can opener konservöppnare
castle slott
cold (illness) förskylning; **(temperature)** kall
comb kam
computer dator
condom kondom
contact lens solution kontaktlinsvätska
corkscrew korkskruv
cup kopp

D

dala horse dalahäst
damage v (damage) skada; n (harm) skada
dance v dansa
dance club diskotek
day ticket dagsbiljett
day trip dagstur
deaf döv
deodorant deodorant
diabetic diabetiker
doll docka

E

each varje
ear öra
earring örhänge
east öster
easy lätt
eat v äta
economy class turist klass
electrical outlet nätuttag
elevator hiss
email e-post

F

family familj
fan (ventilation) fläkt
fantastic adj fantastisk
fare biljettpris
farm bondgård
fast fort
fork gaffel

G

game spel
garbage sopor
garbage bag soppåse
girlfriend flickvän
glass glas
good *adj* bra
gray grått
green grönt

H

hair cut klippning
hair dryer hårtork
hairbrush hårborste
hairdresser damfrisör
hot varm
husband man

I

ice is
icy halt
identification (idenitification) legitimation; **(ID card)** ID-kort
I'd like… Jag skulle vilja ha…
insect repellent mygg olja

J

jacket jacka
jeans jeans
jet ski jetski

K

keep *v* behålla
key nyckel

kiss v kyssa
knife kniv

L

lactose intolerant laktosinterant
ladies' restroom damtoilett
ladieswear damkläder
lake sjö
large stor
lighter tändare
love v älska

M

mail post
mailbox postlåda
manager chef
manicure manikyr
many månqa
map karta
market marknad
married gift
matches tändstickor
medium medium
museum museum

N

nail file nagelfil
nail salon nagelvårdssalong
name n namn
napkin servett
nappy [BE] blöja
nail file nagelfil

napkin servett
nurse sjuksköterska

O

off av
old gammal
on (switch) på
one way (street) enkelriktad
one-way ticket enkel biljett
only bara
open *n* öppet; *v* öppna
opening hours [BE] öppettider
opposite mitt emot
optician optiker
or eller
orange orange

P

pacifier napp
package paket
paddling pool [BE] barnbassäng
pajamas pyjamas
pants byxor
panty hose strumpbyxor
paper napkin papperservett
parcel [BE] paket
park *n* park; *v* parkera
pen kulspetspenna
pink rosa
plate tallrik
purple lila

R

racket (tennis) racket
railroad järnväg
railway [BE] järnväg
rain regn
raincoat regnkappa
rap rap
rape *n* våldtäkt
(disposable) razor (engångs) rakhyvel
razor blades rakblad
red rött

S

safe *n* kassaskåp
sailing segling
sandals sandaler
sanitary napkin binda
saucepan kastrull
sauna bastu
save *v* **(collect)** spara
scarf halsduk
salty salt
sandals sandaler
sanitary napkin binda
sauna bastu
scissors sax
shampoo/conditioner shampoo/hårbalsam
shoes skor
small liten
sneakers träningsskor
snow snö
soap tvål

sock socka
spicy kryddat
spoon sked
stamp *n* frimärke
suitcase resväska
sunglasses solglasögon
sunscreen solskyddskräm
sweater tröja
sweatshirt sweatshirt
swimsuit baddräkt

T

table bord
take *v* ta
taken (occupied) upptagen
tampon tampong
tax skatt
taxi taxi
teaspoon tesked
temperature temperatur
terrible förskräcklig
tie *n* slips
tissues papper näsdukar
toilet paper toalettpapper
toothbrush tandborste
toothpaste tandkräm
tough segt
t-shirt T-skjorta

U

ugly ful
umbrella (standard) paraply; **(sun)** solparasol
underground station [BE] tunnelbanestation
underwear (general) underkläder

V

vacation semester
vacuum cleaner dammsugare
vegetarian vegetarian

W

wait vänta
wake up v vakna
white vitt
wife fru
with med
without utan

Y

yellow gul
yes ja

Z

zoo djurpark

Norwegian

Essentials

Hello/Hi!	**Hallo/Hei!** hah·_loo_´/hay
Goodbye.	**Adjø.** ahd·_yur_´
Yes.	**Ja.** yah
No.	**Nei.** nay
OK.	**OK.** u·_kaw_´
Excuse me.	**Unnskyld.** _ewn_´·shewl
Sorry!	**Beklager!** buh·_klah_´·guhr
I'd like…	**Jeg vil gjerne…** yay vihl _ya_`r·nuh…
How much?	**Hvor mye koster det?**
	voor _mui_`·uh _kohs_`·tuhr _deh_
And/Or	**og/eller** og/eller
Where is/are…?	**Hvor er…?** voor ar…
Please.	**Vær så snill.** var saw snihl
Thank you.	**Takk.** tahk
You're welcome.	**Ingen årsak.** ihng`·uhn _awr_`·sahk
I'm going to…	**Jeg reiser til…** yay _rays_`·uhr tihl…
My name is…	**Jeg heter…** yay _heh_`·tuhr…
Could you speak	**Kan du snakke litt langsommere?** kahn dew
more slowly ?	_snahk_`·kuh liht _lahng_`·sohm·muh·ruh
Could you repeat that?	**Kan du gjenta det?** kahn dew _yehn_´·tah deh
I don't understand.	**Jeg forstår ikke.** yay fohr·_staw_´r ihk`·kuh
Do you speak English?	**Snakker du engelsk?**
	snahk`·kuhr dew _ehng_´·uhlsk
I don't speak (much)	**Jeg snakker ikke (så bra) norsk.**
Norwegian.	yay _snahk_`·kuhr ihk`·kuh (saw brah) nohrsk
Where is the	**Hvor er toalettet?** voor ar tu·ah·_leh_´·tuh
restroom [toilet]?	
Help!	**Hjelp!** yehlp

You'll find the pronunciation of the Norwegian letters and words written in gray after each sentence to guide you. Simply pronounce these as if they were English, noting that any underlines and bolds indicate an additional emphasis or stress or a lengthening of a vowel sound. As you hear the language being spoken, you will quickly become accustomed to the local pronunciation and dialect.

Numbers

0	**null**	*newl*
1	**en**	*ehn*
2	**to**	*too*
3	**tre**	*treh*
4	**fire**	*fee`•ruh*
5	**fem**	*fehm*
6	**seks**	*sehks*
7	**sju**	*shew*
8	**åtte**	*oht`•tuh*
9	**ni**	*nee*
10	**ti**	*tee*
11	**elleve**	*ehl`•vuh*
12	**tolv**	*tohl*
13	**tretten**	*treh`t•tuhn*
14	**fjorten**	*fyu`•rtuhn*
15	**femten**	*fehm`•tuhn*
16	**seksten**	*says`•tuhn*
17	**sytten**	*surt`•tuhn*
18	**atten**	*aht`•tuhn*

YOU MAY SEE...

The Norwegian currency is the **krone** (crown), abbreviated to **kr** or **NOK**, divided into 100 **øre**.
Coins: 50 **øre**; **kr** 1, 5, 10 and 20
Notes: **kr** 50, 100, 200, 500 and 1,000

Cash can be obtained from **minibank** (ATMs), which can be readily found in urban areas. ATMs offer good rates, though there may be hidden fees.

Money can be exchanged at **Vekslingskontor** (currency exchange offices), banks and post offices. These can be found at airports, train stations, ship terminals and in many tourist centers.

Banks are generally open Monday to Friday from 8:15 a.m. to 3:30 p.m., though some close later one day a week and hours may vary in smaller towns. Remember to bring your passport for identification.

I'd like to change some dollars/pounds.	**Jeg vil gjerne veksle noen dollar/pund.** *yay vihl ya`r•nuh vehk`s•luh noo`•uhn dohl´•lahr/pewn*
I'd like to cash a traveler's check [cheque].	**Jeg vil gjerne løse inn en reisesjekk.** *yay vihl ya`r• nuh lur`•suh ihn ehn ray`•suh•shehk*
Can I pay in cash?	**Kan jeg betale kontant?** *kahn yay buh•tah´•luh kun•tahn´t*
Can I pay by credit card?	**Kan jeg betale med kredittkort?** *kahn yay buh•tah´•luh meh kreh•diht´•kohrt*

For Numbers, see page 118.

124

Getting Around

How do I get to town?	**Hvordan kommer jeg til byen?** *voor´•dahn kohm´•muhr yay tihl bui´•uhn*
Where is…?	**Hvor er…?** *voor ar…*
the airport	**flyplassen** *flui´•plahs•suhn*
the train station	**jernbanestasjonen** *ya`rn•bah•nuh•stah•shoon•uhn*
the bus station	**busstasjonen** *bews´•stah•shoon•uhn*

the subway [underground] station	**T-banestasjonen** *teh´·bah·nuh·stah·shoon·uhn*
How far is it?	**Hvor langt er det?** *voor lahngt ar deh*
Where can I buy tickets?	**Hvor kan jeg kjøpe billetter?** *voor kahn yay khur`·puh bihl·leht´·tuhr*
A one-way [single]/ round-trip [return] ticket.	**En enveisbillett/tur-returbillett.** *ehn ehn´·vays·bihl·leht/tewr·reh·tew´r·bil·leht*
How much?	**Hvor mye koster det?** *voor mui`·uh kohs`·tuhr deh*

Norway runs a train network more than 4,000 km (c. 2,500 miles) long, though the system is much more comprehensive in the south than the north. Oslo is the main hub for most long-distance, express and local trains. Long-distance lines that span the country are an excellent way to view the incredible Norwegian scenery. A number of discounts are available: children under 4 travel free of charge, and children under 16 and senior citizens travel at half price. Local buses, trams, subways and ferries run on an integrated network, so you can transfer for no additional cost. Keep in mind that buying a **flexikort** (multi-trip ticket) is cheaper than buying single tickets. For moving around the capital, you may also want to consider a 1-, 2- or 3-day (children's or family) **Oslo Pass**, which offers unlimited public transportation within greater Oslo and free entry to a number of museums and tourist attractions. For long-distance travel, passes such as Eurorail (non-European residents), InterRail (European residents) or ScanRail (for travel within Scandinavia) can offer better value fares.

Ferry and boat travel is efficient in Norway. Most ferries and high-speed ships have frequent departure schedules, so you rarely have to wait in lines, and the cost for passenger and car transport is generally low. Besides regular ferry service, several companies offer cruises along the fjords. These are very popular during the summer months and tickets are more expensive during this period, so reservations should be made well in advance.

Which...?	**Hvilken...?** _vihl´•kuhn..._
gate	**utgang** _ew`t•gahng_
line	**linje** _lihn`•yuh_
platform	**perrong** _pehr•rohng´_
Where can I get a taxi?	**Hvor kan jeg få tak i en drosje?** _voor kahn yay faw tahk ih ehn drohsh`•uh_
Can you take me to this address?	**Kan du kjøre meg til denne adressen?** _kahn dew khur`•ruh may tihl dehn`•nuh ahd•rehs´•suhn_
To...Airport, please.	**Til...lufthavn.** _tihl... lewft´•hahvn_
I'm in a hurry.	**Jeg har dårlig tid.** _yay hahr dawr`•lih teed_
Can I have a map?	**Kan jeg få et kart?** _kahn yay faw eht kahrt_

If you enjoy cycling there are many well-planned routes throughout the country, through lush valleys and breathtaking fjords. Attractions are usually signposted. You can bring your own bike or rent one easily. Given the terrain, a **terrengsykkel** (mountain bike) is usually the most practical option.

Tickets

When's...to Stavanger?	**Når går...til Stavanger?** *nohr gawr...tihl stah•vahng´•uhr*
the (first) bus	**(første) buss** *(furrs`•tuh) bews*
the (next) flight	**(neste) fly** *(nehs`•tuh) flui*
the (last) train	**(siste) tog** *(sihs`•tuh) tawg*
One ticket/ please.	**En billett/To billetter, takk.** *ehn bihl•leht´/too bihl•leht´•tuhr tak*
For today/tomorrow.	**For i dag/i morgen.** *fohr ih•dahg/ih•mawr`•uhn*

127

The Oslo **Tunnelbane** or **T-bane** (subway) runs from approximately 5:30 a.m. to just after midnight. Buying a **flexikort** (multi-trip ticket) is a good idea if you plan on making numerous trips. It can be used to make transfers within one hour at no extra charge. An **Oslo Pass** is another discount travel pass, good for all forms of public transportation.

NORDLYS
TROMSØ

Norwegian

Essentials

A one-way [single]/ round-trip [return] ticket.	**En enveisbillett/tur-returbillett.** *ehn ehn ´·vays·bihl·leht/tewr·reh·tew´r·bil·leht*
A first class/economy class ticket.	**En billett på første klasse/turistklasse.** *ehn bihl·eht´ poh furrs`·tuh klahs`·suh/ tew·rihst´·klahs·suh*
I have an e-ticket.	**Jeg har en e-billett.** *yay hahr ehn eh´·bihl·leht*
How long is the trip?	**Hvor lang er turen?** *voor lang ar tew´·ruhn*
Is it a direct train?	**Går toget direkte?** *gawr tawg·eht deeh·rehk·teh*
Can you tell me when to get off?	**Kan du si meg når jeg skal av?** *kahn dew see may nohr yay skahl ah*

128

Taxis can be hailed in the street, found at taxi stands or ordered
by phone. All cabs are metered and service charges are included
in the fare. You can tip the driver by rounding up the fare. Keep in
mind that rates differ from place to place and travel by taxi is generally
expensive, so ask for an approximate fare beforehand. Most taxis accept
credit cards but be sure to double check first.

I'd like to…my reservation.	**Jeg vil gjerne…reservasjonen.**
	yay vihl ya`r•nuh…reh•sehr•vah•shoo´n•uhn
cancel	**annullere** *ahn•newl•leh´•ruh*
change	**endre** *ehn`•druh*
confirm	**bekrefte** *buh•krehf´•tuh*

For Time, see page 120.

Car Hire

Where can I rent a car?	**Hvor kan jeg leie en bil?**
	voor kahn yay lay`•uh ehn beel
I'd like to rent [hire]…	**Jeg vil gjerne leie…**
	yay vihl ya`r•nuh lay`•uh…
an automatic	**en bil med automatgir** *meh ev•tu•mah´t•geer*
a car with air conditioning	**en bil med klimaanlegg** *ehn beel meh klee´•mah•ahn•lehg*

YOU MAY HEAR…

rett frem *reht frehm*	straight ahead
på venstre side *poh vehn´•struh see`•duh*	on the left
på høyre side *poh hury´•ruh see`•duh*	on the right
på/rundt hjørnet *poh/rewnt yurr´•nuh*	on/around the corner
midt imot… *miht ih•moot´…*	opposite…
bak… *bahk…*	behind…
ved siden av… *veh see`•duhn ah…*	next to…
etter… *eht`•tuhr…*	after…
nord/sør *noor/surr*	north/south
øst/vest *urst/vehst*	east/west
ved lyskrysset *veh lui`s•kruis•suh*	at the traffic light
ved veikrysset *veh vay`•kruis•suh*	at the intersection

a car seat	**et barnesete** *eht bahr`·nuh·seh·tuh*
a cheap/small car	**en billig/liten bil** *ehn bihl·ih/liht·ehn beel*
How much…?	**Hvor mye koster det…?**
	voor mui`·uh kohs`·tuhr deh…
per day	**per dag** *pehr dahg*
per week	**per uke** *pehr ew`·kuh*
Are there any discounts?	**Er det noen rabatter?** *ar deh noo`·uhn rah·baht´·tuhr*

130

Parking in Norway is restricted, particularly on weekdays. The most common system is the **P-automat** (automated parking meter) when you park your car, then pay for an amount of time at the meter; the meter then prints a ticket to be displayed on your dashboard. Another option is a **P-hus** (parking garage) when you receive a ticket upon entering the garage. Before getting into your car to leave the garage, you must pay for your ticket at an automated machine or a manned booth.

If you didn't reserve a room before your arrival, the local tourist office can provide information and help you to arrange a reservation. The official website of the Norwegian Tourist Board, Visit Norway (www.visitnorway.com), can provide information about locations in particular cities.

Places to Stay

Can you recommend a hotel?	**Kan du anbefale et hotell?** kahn dew ahn´•buh•**fah**•luh eht hu•<u>tehl</u>´
I have a reservation.	**Jeg har bestilt rom.** yay hahr buh•<u>stihlt</u>´ rum
My name is...	**Jeg heter...** yay <u>heh</u>`•tuhr...
Do you have a room...?	**Har dere et rom...?** hahr deh`•ruh eht rum...
for one/two	**for én/to** fohr ehn/too
with a bathroom	**med bad** meh bahd
with air conditioning	**med klimaanlegg** meh <u>klee</u>´•mah•ahn•lehg
For tonight.	**For i natt.** fohr ih naht

In Norway, there are a variety of accommodation alternatives in addition to more conventional options such as hotels, bed and breakfasts or **husrom** (rooms in private houses) and **vandrerhjem** (hostels). For a unique holiday experience you could consider a **bondegårdsferie** (farm stay), which lets you taste Norwegian farm life firsthand. Similarly, along the coast, you could arrange to stay in **rorbuer** (fisherman's cabins). **Hytter** (chalets or cabins) are available throughout the country as well.

For two nights.	**For to netter.** *fohr t*oo *neht´·tuhr*
For one week.	**For en uke.** *fohr ehn ew`·kuh*
How much?	**Hvor mye koster det?** *voor mui`·uh kohs`·tuhr deh*
Do you have anything cheaper?	**Har dere noe rimeligere?** *hahr deh`·ruh noo`·uh ree`·muh·lih·uh·ruh*
When's check-out?	**Når må jeg sjekke ut?** *nohr maw yay shehk`·kuh ewt*

Can I leave this in the safe?	**Kan jeg legge denne/dette igjen i safen?** *kahn yay lehg`-guh dehn`-nuh/ deht`-tuh ih•yehn` ih sayf`-uhn*
Can I leave my bags?	**Kan jeg sette igjen bagasjen?** *kahn yay seht`-tuh ih•yehn` bah•gah`-shuhn*
Can I have the bill/ a receipt?	**Kan jeg få regningen/en kvittering?** *kahn yay faw ray`-ning-uhn/ehn kviht•teh`-rihng*
I'll pay in cash/by credit card.	**Jeg betaler kontant/med kredittkort.** *yay buh•tah`-luhr kun•tahnt`/meh kreh•diht`-kohrt*

Communications

Where's an internet cafe?	**Hvor finner jeg en internettkafé?** *voor fihn`-nuhr yay ehn ihn`-tuhr•neht•kah•feh`*
Can I access the internet/check e-mail?	**Kan jeg bruke internett/sjekke e-post?** *kahn yay brew`-kuh ihn`-tuhr•neht/ shehk`-kuh eh`-pohst*
How much per hour/ half hour?	**Hvor mye er det for en time/halv time?** *voor mui`-uh ar deh fohr ehn tee`-muh/ hahl tee`-muh*
How do I connect/ log on?	**Hvordan kobler jeg meg opp/logger jeg meg inn?** *voor`-dahn kohb`-luhr yay may ohp/lohg`-guhr yay may ihn*

Norwegians tend to get right to business and don't tend to engage in much small talk or socializing. You'll find them to be serious and direct in business dealings, and in their manner of speaking in general.

Though titles and surnames are used frequently in introductions, they are usually dropped later. Greetings are accompanied by a handshake.

Can I have a phone card?	**Kan jeg få et telefonkort?** *kahn yay faw eht teh•luh•foon´•kohrt*
Can I have your phone number?	**Kan jeg få telefonnummeret ditt?** *kahn yay faw teh•luh•foon´•num•muhr•uh diht*
Here's my number/ email address.	**Her har du nummeret mitt/e-postadressen min.** *har hahr dew num´•muhr•uh miht/ eh´•pohst•ahd•rehs•suhn mihn*
Call me.	**Ring meg.** *rihng may*
Can you text me?	**Kan du sende meg en tekstmelding?** *kahn dew sehn`•nuh may ehn tehkst´•mehl•lihng*
I'll text you.	**Jeg sender deg en tekstmelding.** *yay sehn`•nuhr day ehn tehkst´•mehl•lihng*
Email me.	**Send meg en e-post.** *sehn may ehn eh´•pohst*
Hello. This is…	**Hallo. Dette er…** *hah•loo´ deht`•tuh ar…*
I'd like to speak to…	**Kan jeg få snakke med…?** *kahn yay faw snahk`•kuh meh…*
Can you repeat that?	**Kan du gjenta det?** *kahn dew yehn´•tah deh*
I'll call back later.	**Jeg ringer igjen senere.** *yay rihng`•uhr ih•yehn´ seh`•nuh•ruh*
Goodbye.	**Adjø.** *ahd•yur´*
Where's the post office?	**Hvor er postkontoret?** *voor ar pohst´•kun•toor•uh*
Can I send this to…?	**Kan jeg få sendt dette til…?** *kahn yay faw sehnt deht`•tuh tihl…*
Can I…?	**Kan jeg…?** *kahn yay…*
access the Internet	**bruke internett** *brew`•kuh ihn´•tuhr•neht*
check email	**sjekke e-post** *shehk`•kuh eh´•pohst*
print	**skrive ut** *skree`•vuh ewt*

plug in/charge my laptop/iPhone/iPad/BlackBerry?	**koble til/lade min bærbare maskin/iPhone/iPad/BlackBerry?** *kawb•leh tihl/lah•deh mihn bar•bahr•eh mah•sheen/ay•foan/ay•pad/blahk•behr•ree*
access Skype?	**bruke Skype** *brew•keh skayp*
What is the WiFi password?	**Hva er WiFi-passordet?** *vah ar vee•fee•pahs•ur•eht*
Is the WiFi free?	**Er WiFi gratis?** *ar vee•fee grah•tihs*
Do you have bluetooth?	**Har dere bluetooth?** *hahr dehr•eh blew•tewth*
Do you have a scanner?	**Har dere en skanner?** *hahr dehr•eh ehn skahn•ehr*

Social Media

Are you on Facebook/Twitter?	**Er du på Facebook/Twitter?** *ar dew paw feis•bewk/tviht•ehr*
What's your user name?	**Hva er brukernavnet ditt?** *vah ar brewk•ehr•nahvn•eht diht*
I'll add you as a friend.	**Jeg legger deg til som venn.** *yay lehg•ehr day tihl sawm vehn*

I'll follow you on Twitter.	**Jeg følger deg på Twitter.** *yay furl•ehr day paw tviht•ehr*
Are you following...?	**Følger du...?** *furl•her dew*
I'll put the pictures on Facebook/Twitter.	**Jeg legger ut bildene på Facebook/Twitter.** *yay lehg•ehr ewt bihl•deh•neh paw feis•bewk/ tviht•ehr*
I'll tag you in the pictures.	**Jeg tagger deg i bildene.** *yay tag•ehr day ee bihl•dehn•eh*

Conversation

Hello/Hi!	**Hallo/Hei!** *hah•loo´/hay*
How are you?	**Hvordan står det til?** *voor´•dahn stawr deh tihl*
Fine, thanks.	**Bare bra, takk.** *bah`•ruh brah tahk*

De (the formal form of 'you') is generally no longer used to address strangers, but is restricted to written works and addressing older people. As a general rule, **du** can be used in all situations without offending anyone.

Excuse me.	**Unnskyld.** _ewn´•shewl_	
Do you speak English?	**Snakker du engelsk?**	
	snahk`•kuhr dew ehng´•ehlsk	
What's your name?	**Hva heter du?** _vah heh`•tuhr dew_	
My name is…	**Jeg heter…** _yay heh´•tuhr…_	
Nice to meet you!	**Hyggelig å treffes!** _huig`•guh•lih aw trehf`•fuhs_	
Where are you from?	**Hvor kommer du fra?**	
	voor kohm´•muhr dew frah	
I'm from the U.S./	**Jeg er fra USA/Storbritannia.** _yay ar frah_	137
the U.K.	_ew•ehs•ah´/stoo´r•brih•tahn•yah_	
What do you do?	**Hva jobber du med?** _vah yohb`•buhr dew meh_	
I work for…	**Jeg jobber for…** _yay yohb`•buhr fohr…_	
I'm a student.	**Jeg er student.** _yay ar stew•dehnt´_	
I'm retired.	**Jeg er pensjonist.** _yay ar pang•shu•nihst´_	

Romance

Would you like to go out for a drink/meal?	**Skal vi gå og ta en drink/ut og spise?** *skahl vee gaw oh tah ehn dringk/ewt oh spee`·suh*
What are your plans for tonight/tomorrow?	**Hva gjør du i kveld/i morgen?** *vah yurr dew ih kvehl/ih maw`·ruhn*
Can I have your number?	**Kan jeg få nummeret ditt?** *kahn yay faw num´·muhr·uh diht*
Can I join you?	**Er det opptatt her?** *ar deh awp·that har*
Can I buy you a drink?	**Kan jeg by på en drink?** *kahn yay bui poh ehn drihngk*
I love you.	**Jeg elsker deg.** *yay ehls`·kuhr day*

Accepting & Rejecting

I'd love to, thanks.	**Takk, det vil jeg gjerne.** *tahk deh vihl yay ya`r·nuh*
Where should we meet?	**Hvor skal vi møtes?** *voor skahl vee mur`·tuhs*
Let's meet at the bar/your hotel.	**Vi møtes i baren/på hotellet ditt.** *vee mur`·tuhs ee bah´·ruhn/poh hu·tehl´·luh diht*
I'll come by at…	**Jeg henter deg…** *yay hehn`·tuhr day…*
Thanks, but I'm busy.	**Takk, men jeg er dessverre opptatt.** *tahk mehn yay ar dehs·vehr´·ruh ohp´·taht*
I'm not interested.	**Jeg er ikke interessert.** *yay ar ihk`·kuh ihn·truhs·seh´rt*
Leave me alone.	**Vær så snill å la meg være i fred.** *var soh snihl oh lah may va`·ruh ih freh*
Stop bothering me!	**Slutt å plage meg!** *slewt oh plah`·guh may*

Food & Drink

Eating Out

Can you recommend a good restaurant/bar? **Kan du anbefale en bra restaurant/bar?** *kahn d**ew** ahn´•buh•**fah**•luh ehn br**a**h rehs•tew•**rahng**´/b**a**hr*

Is there a traditional Norwegian/an inexpensive restaurant near here? **Fins det en typisk norsk/billig restaurant i nærheten?** *fihns deh ehn t**ui**´•pihsk nohrsk/**bihl**`•lih rehs•tew•**rahng**´ ih n**ar**´•heh•tuhn*

A table for... **Et bord til...** *eht b**oo**r tihl...*

Could we have a table here/there? **Kan vi få et bord her/der?** *kahn **vee faw** eht eht b**oo**r har/dar*

Could we have a table in the corner? **Kan vi få et hjørnebord?** *kahn **vee faw** eht eht **yur**`•n•uh•b**oo**r*

I'm waiting for someone. **Jeg venter på noen.** *yay **vehn**`•tuhr poh **noo**`•uhn*

Where is the restroom [toilet]? **Hvor er toalettet?** *voor ar tu•ah•**leht**´•tuh*

Food & Drink

Can I have a menu?	**Kan jeg få se menyen?**
	kahn yay faw seh meh•nui´•uhn
What do you recommend?	**Hva kan du anbefale?**
	vah kahn dew ahn´•buh•fah•luh
I'd like…	**Jeg vil gjerne ha…** *yay vihl ya`r•nuh hah…*
Can I have more…?	**Kan jeg få litt mer…?**
	kahn yay faw liht mehr…
Enjoy your meal!	**God appetitt!** *gu ahp•puh•tiht´*
Can I have the check [bill]?	**Kan jeg få regningen?**
	kahn yay faw ray`•nihng•uhn

Norwegian cuisine features a wide range of soups, which are often eaten with **flatbrød** (a thin, barley and wheat or barley and rye cracker); this is a common starter. **Fiskesuppe** (fish soup) is very popular along the coast. Other traditional soups involve meat, such as **betasuppe** (meat and vegetable soup), or vegetables, like **gul ertesuppe** (yellow pea soup).

Is service included?	**Er service inkludert?**	
	ar surr´·vihs ing·klew·dehrt´	
Can I pay by credit card?	**Kan jeg betale med kredittkort?** *kahn yay buh·tah´·luh meh kreh·diht´·kohrt*	
Can I have a receipt?	**Kan jeg få kvittering?**	
	kahn yay faw kviht·teh´·rihng	
Thank you.	**Takk.** *tahk*	

Breakfast

bacon *bay´·kuhn*	bacon
brød *brur*	bread
smør *smurr*	butter
ost *ust*	cheese
egg *ehg*	eggs
bløtkokt/hardkokt egg	soft-boiled/hard-boiled eggs
blur`t·kukt/hah`r·kukt ehg	
speilegg *spayl`·ehg*	fried egg
eggerøre *ehg`·guh·rur·ruh*	scrambled eggs
syltetøy *suil`·tuh·tury*	jam
omelett *oh·muh·leht´*	omelet

Frokost (breakfast) is usually eaten early and consists of coffee or tea and **smørbrød** (open-faced sandwiches) and perhaps cereal. **Lunsj** (lunch) is typically a light meal and may consist of a simple **matpakke** (open-faced sandwich brought from home). **Middag** (dinner) is often the only hot meal of the day. If **middag** is eaten early, then **aftens** (a late night snack), consisting of bread or crackers with butter or cheese and cold cuts, is eaten to get through the night without going hungry.

ristet brød _rihs`_·tuht b**rur**	toast
yoghurt _yoo´_·gewrt	yogurt
pølse _purl`_·suh	sausage

Appetizers

blåskjell _blaw`_·shehl	mussels
fiskesuppe _fihs`_·kuh·sewp·puh	fish soup
grønnsaksuppe _grurn`_·s**ahk**·sewp·puh	vegetable soup
gravlaks _grahv´_·lahks	cured salmon flavored with dill
hummer _hum´_·muhr	lobster
tomatsuppe tu·_mah´t_·sewp·puh	tomato soup
kjøttsuppe _khurt`_·sewp·puh	meat soup
sursild _sewr´sihl_	marinated herring
østers _urs´_·tehrs	oysters

A 10-15% service charge is typically included in most restaurant bills, though wait staff often receive an extra 5-10% tip.

Wolffish
Monkfish
Filet of reindeer
Whalesteak
Medallion of elk

Meat

oksekjøtt <u>ohk</u>`·suh·khurt	beef
kylling <u>khuil</u>`·lihng	chicken
lammekjøtt <u>lahm</u>`·muh·khurt	lamb
svinekjøtt <u>svee</u>`·nuh·khurt	pork
biff bihf	beef steak
kalvekjøtt <u>kahl</u>`·vuh·khurt	veal

Fish & Seafood

torsk tohrsk	cod
sild sihl	herring
hummer <u>hum</u>´·muhr	lobster
laks lahks	salmon
reker <u>reh</u>`·kuhr	shrimp [prawns]

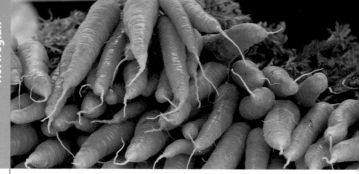

Vegetables

bønner _burn`•nuhr_	beans
kål _kawl_	cabbage
gulrøtter _gew`l•rurt•tuhr_	carrots
sopp _sohp_	mushrooms
løk _lurk_	onions
erter _ehr´•tuhr_	peas
potet _pu•teh´t_	potato
tomater _tu•maht´•uhr_	tomatoes

Sauces & Condiments

pepper	**pepper** _pehp´•puhr_
salt	**salt** _sahlt_
ketchup	**ketchup** _kat•shewp_
mustard	**sennep** _sehn•ehp_

In Norway, there are a few large supermarket chains, such as Rimi, Rema and Kiwi, in addition to many local mini-markets. Keep in mind that supermarkets do not accept credit cards, so remember to bring cash when you go shopping for groceries.

Measurements in Europe are metric - and that applies to the weight of food too. If you tend to think in pounds and ounces, it's worth brushing up on what the metric equivalent is before you go shopping for fruit and veg in markets and supermarkets. Five hundred grams, or half a kilo, is a common quantity to order, and that converts to just over a pound (17.65 ounces, to be precise).

Fruit & Dessert

eple _ehp`·luh_	apple
banan _bah·nah´n_	banana
sitron _siht·roo´n_	lemon
appelsin _ahp·puhl·see´n_	orange
pære _pa`·ruh_	pear
jordbær _yoo´r·bar_	strawberries
is _ees_	ice cream
pannekaker _pahn`·nuh·kah·kuhr_	pancakes
sjokolade _shu·ku·lah`·duh_	chocolate
bløtkake _blur`t·kah·kuh_	layer cake
varm eplekake med krem _vahrm ehp`·luh·kah·kuh meh krehm_	hot apple pie with whipped cream
mandelkake _mahn´·duhl·kah·kuh_	almond cake
tyttebær _tuit´·tuh·bar_	lingonberry

Drinks

Can I have the wine list/drink menu?	**Kan jeg få se vinkartet/drikkekartet?** _kahn yay faw seh veen`·kahr·tuh/drihk`·kuh·kahr·tuh_
What do you recommend?	**Hva kan du anbefale?** _vah kahn dew ahn´·buh·fah·luh_

Can I have the house wine?	**Kan jeg få husets vin?** *kahn yay faw <u>hew</u>´s•uhs veen*
Can I buy you a drink?	**Kan jeg by på en drink?** *kahn yay bui poh ehn drihngk*
Cheers!	**Skål!** *skawl*
A coffee/tea, please.	**En kaffe/te, takk.** *ehn <u>kahf</u>´•fuh/teh tahk*

Beer in Norway is classified by strength. **Lettøl** (beer with low alcohol content) is less than 2.5% alcohol content and **zero** and **vørterøl** are both non-alcoholic. **Pils** (lager) and **bayerøl** (medium-strength dark beer) are relatively low in alcohol content. The strongest beers (6-10%), like **eksportøl** (strong light beer) and **bokkøl** (strong dark beer), are only sold at the **Vinmonopolet** (state-run liquor store). If you are in Norway around Christmas time, be sure to try some of the special limited-edition Christmas brews which are extremely popular with the locals.

Beer, in addition to being drunk on its own, often serves as a chaser to **akevitt** (aquavit), an extremely potent drink distilled from potato and caraway seeds.

If you're not in the mood for Norwegian beer or spirits, there are a number of other drinks to enjoy. Tea and especially strong coffee are commonly drunk throughout the day. For soft drinks you could try **Solo** (orange-flavored soda) or **Mozell** (apple-flavored soda).

Black.	**Svart.** *svahrt*	
With...	**Med...** *meh...*	
milk	**melk** *mehlk*	
sugar	**sukker** <u>*suk*</u>´*·kuhr*	
artificial sweetener	**søtningsmiddel** <u>*sur*</u>`*t·nihngs·mihd·duhl*	
A glass of..., please.	**Et glass..., takk.** *eht glahs...tahk*	
juice	**juice** *yews*	
soda	**soda** <u>*soo*</u>´*·dah*	
(sparkling/still) water	**vann (med kullsyre/uten kullsyre)** *vahn (meh* <u>*kewl*</u>`*·sui·ruh/*<u>*ew*</u>`*·tuhn* <u>*kewl*</u>`*·sui·ruh)*	
Is the tap water safe to drink?	**Kan man drikke vann rett fra springen?** *kahn mahn* <u>*drihk*</u>`*·kuh vahn reht frah* <u>*sprihng*</u>´*·uhn*	

DET HANSEATISKE MUSEUM

Culturally, there is a lot to enjoy in Norway. In summer, many cultural events, including orchestral concerts and operas, are celebrated outdoors. Theater is extremely popular, though most productions are in Norwegian. Classical ballet is performed at the Oslo Opera House and traditional folk dances can be seen across the country. If you are interested in the visual arts, the Munch museum, named after the internationally-famous Edvard Munch, in Oslo is popular. The extensive National Museum of Art, Architecture and Design is also in Oslo.

Leisure Time

Sightseeing

Where's the tourist information office?
Hvor er turistkontoret? *voor ar tew•rihst´•kun•too•ruh*

What are the main points of interest?
Hva er de viktigste severdighetene? *vah ar dih vihk`•tik•stuh seh•vehr´•dih•heh•tuh•nuh*

| Do you have tours in English? | **Har dere omvisninger på engelsk?** *hahr deh`·ruh ohm´·vihs·nihng·uhr poh ehng´·uhlsk* |
| Can I have a map/guide? | **Kan jeg få et kart/en guide?** *kahn yay faw eht kahrt/ehn gied* |

Shopping

Where is the market/mall [shopping centre]?	**Hvor er torget/kjøpesenteret?** *voor ar tohr´·guh/khur`·puh·sehn·truh*
I'm just looking.	**Jeg bare ser meg omkring.** *yay bah`·ruh sehr may ohm·krihng´*
Can you help me?	**Kan du hjelpe meg?** *kahn dew yehl`·puh may*
I'm being helped.	**Jeg får hjelp.** *yay fawr yehlp*

Norway offers shopping choices for a range of budgets. Even in the capital, a good deal of shopping can be done on foot. Many of the major stores are located in the area around **Karl Johans** gate and on **Bogstadveien** and **Hegdehaugsveien** streets. **Grünerløkka** is the place to go to find trendy boutiques showcasing the work of young Norwegian designers. Here you'll also find lots of second-hand shops, music stores and independent stores selling local pottery and handicrafts. For everything under one roof in Oslo, visit **Aker Brygge**, **Byporten**, **Glasmagasinet**, **Oslo City**, **Paleet**, **Steen & Strøm** and **Vikaterrassen**.

Regular store hours are Monday to Friday from 9:00 a.m. to 5:00 p.m. (on Saturday to 3:00 p.m.), but many stores stay open later. Shopping malls are generally open Monday to Friday from 10:00 a.m. to 9:00 p.m. and Saturday from 9:00 a.m. to 6:00 p.m. Most stores are closed on Sunday.

How much?	**Hvor mye koster det?**
	voor mew`·uh kohs`·tuhr deh
That one.	**Den der.** *dehn dar*
No, thanks. That's all.	**Nei takk. Det var alt.** *nay tahk deh vahr ahlt*
Where do I pay?	**Hvor betaler man?** *voor buh·tah´·luhr mahn*
I'll pay in cash/by	**Jeg betaler kontant/med kredittkort.** *yay*
credit card.	*buh·tah´·luhr kun·tahn´t/meh kreh·diht´·kohrt*
Could I have a receipt?	**Kan jeg få kvittering?**
	kahn yay faw kviht·teh´·rihng

Typical souvenirs from Norway include knit items like sweaters
and cardigans, gloves and mittens. Other handcrafted pieces like
silver, glassware, pottery and hand-painted wooden objects, such as
bowls with rose designs, Norwegian trolls, fjord horses and viking ships
abound. Art lovers will find that there are also many art galleries across
the country. It is a good idea to get local recommendations on where to
buy. Goat and reindeer skins as well as furs are also popular.

Tourist offices are located throughout Norway. The local tourist office can provide information for visitors on accommodation, activities and other entertainment. Visit Norway, the official website of the Norwegian Tourist Board, www.visitnorway.com, can provide information about locations in particular cities.

Sport & Leisure

When's the game?	**Når går kampen?**	nohr gawr <u>kahm´</u>•puhn
Where's...?	**Hvor er...?**	voor ar...
the beach	**stranden**	<u>strahn´</u>•nuhn
the park	**parken**	<u>pahr´</u>•kuhn

On good summer days the temperatures in Norway can be warm enough to sunbathe and swim. There are possibilities for diving, waterskiing and windsurfing along the coast and on Norway's many lakes. White-water rafting and kayaking are an adrenaline-pumping option on the rivers in Oppland, Hedmark and Sør-Trøndelag.

the swimming pool **svømmebassenget**

svurm`•muh•bahs•sehng•uh

Is it safe to swim/ dive here?	**Er det trygt å svømme/dykke her?** <u>*ar*</u> *deh truikt aw svurm`•muh/<u>duik</u>`•kuh har*
Can I rent [hire] golf clubs?	**Kan jeg leie golfkøller?** *kahn yay <u>lay</u>`•uh <u>gohlf</u>´•kurl•luhr*

Norwegians are very active people and particularly enjoy outdoor sports. Water sports, such as boating, canoeing and fishing are popular, though skiing and hiking are the primary participant sports. In fact, Norwegians boast 4,000 years of skiing, since skis were originally developed as a means of transportation through the snow. Today, there are many ski resorts across Norway and tourist offices can recommend the nearest one for downhill skiing as well as local ski facilities for cross-country skiing. Hiking can be done almost anywhere, but if you're up for an exhilarating experience, try **brevandringer** (guided glacier walks).

How much per hour?	**Hvor mye koster det per time?**	
	voor mui`•uh kohs`•tuhr deh pehr tee`•muh	
How far is it to…?	**Hvor langt er det til…?**	
	voor lahngt´ar deh tihl…	
Can you show me on the map?	**Kan du vise meg det på kartet?** *kahn dew*	
	vee`•suh may deh poh kahr´•tuh	

Going Out

What is there to do at night?	**Hva kan man gjøre om kvelden?** *vah kahn mahn*	
	yur`•ruh ohm kvehl´•uhn	
Do you have a program of events?	**Har du en oversikt over ting som skjer?** *hahr dew*	
	ehn aw`•vuhr•sihkt aw´•vuhr tihng sohm shehr	
What's playing at the movies [cinema] tonight?	**Hvilke filmer vises på kino i kveld?** *vihl`•kuh*	
	fihl`•muhr vee`•suhs poh khee`•nu ih kvehl	

Oslo offers endless options for going out in pubs, bars, cafes and nightclubs. Many clubs offer live music and attract DJs and musicians from around the world. Oslo also has a growing jazz scene. All restaurants, bars and nightclubs are smoke-free indoors, though many set up outdoor tables in summer and protection for smokers in the winter. Keep in mind that alcohol is considerably more expensive in Norway than in other countries and many clubs enforce age restrictions.

Where's...?	**Hvor er...?** *voor ar...*
the downtown area	**sentrum** *sehn´·trewm*
the bar	**baren** *bahr´·uhn*
the dance club	**diskoteket** *dihs·ku·teh´·kuh*
What's the admission charge?	**Hva koster det å komme inn?** *vah kohs`·tuhr deh oh kohm`·muh ihn*
Is this area safe at night?	**Er dette området trygt om natten?** *ar deht·eh awm·rawd·eht trygt awm naht·ehn*

Baby Essentials

Do you have…?	**Har dere…?** *hahr <u>deh</u>`·ruh…*	
a baby bottle	**en tåteflaske** *ehn <u>taw</u>`·tuh·flahs·kuh*	
baby wipes	**papirkluter** *pah·<u>pee</u>´r·klew·tuhr*	
a car seat	**et barnesete** *eht <u>bahr</u>`·nuh·seh·tuh*	
a children's menu/ portion	**en barnemeny/barneporsjon** *ehn <u>bahr</u>`·nuh· meh·**nui**/<u>bahr</u>`·nuh·poor·shoon*	
a child's seat/ highchair	**en barnestol/babystol** *ehn <u>bahr</u>`·nuh·stool/ <u>beh</u>´·bih·stool*	
a crib/cot	**en barneseng/sprinkelseng** *ehn <u>bahr</u>`·nuh·sehng/<u>sprihng</u>´·kul·sehng*	
diapers [nappies]	**bleier** *<u>blay</u>`·uhr*	
formula	**morsmelkerstatning** *<u>moors</u>´·mehlk·ehr·staht·nihng*	
a pacifier [dummy]	**en narresmokk** *ehn <u>nahr</u>`·ruh·smuk*	
a playpen	**en lekegrind** *ehn <u>leh</u>`·kuh·grihn*	
a stroller [pushchair]	**en gåstol** *ehn <u>gaw</u>´·stool*	

| Can I breastfeed the baby here? | **Kan jeg amme babyen her?** *kahn yay <u>ahm</u>`•uh b<u>eh</u>´•bih•uhn h<i>a</i>r* |
| Where can I change the baby? | **Hvor kan jeg bytte på babyen?** *voor kahn yay <u>buit</u>`•tuh poh b<u>eh</u>´•bih•uhn* |

Major credit cards are accepted at most hotels, restaurants, large shops, car rental companies and airlines, though some places will not accept them, particularly supermarkets and gas stations. It is a good idea to have some cash on hand, just in case. Traveler's checks are less widely used these days and are best cashed in a bank or Post Office.

Disabled Travelers

Is there...?	**Er det...?** *ar deh...*	
access for the disabled	**adkomst for bevegelseshemmede** *ahd`•kohmst fohr buh•<u>veh</u>´•guhl•suhs•hem•muhd•uh*	
a wheelchair ramp	**en rullestolsrampe** *ehn <u>rewl</u>`•luh•stools•rahm•puh*	
a handicapped-[disabled-] accessible toilet	**et handikaptoalett** *eht <u>hehn</u>´•dih•kehp•tu•ah•leht*	
I need...	**Jeg trenger...** *yay <u>trehng</u>´•uhr...*	
assistance	**hjelp** *yehlp*	
an elevator [lift]	**en heis** *ehn hays*	
a ground-floor room	**et rom i første etasje** *eht rum ih <u>furr</u>`•stuh eh•<u>tah</u>´•shuh*	
Can you speak louder/more slowly?	**Kan du snakke litt høyere/langsommere?** *kahn dew <u>snahk</u>`•kuh liht <u>hury</u>`•uhr•uh/ <u>lahng</u>`•sohm•muhr•uh*	

Health & Emergencies

Emergencies

Help!	**Hjelp!** *yehlp*
Go away!	**Gå vekk!** *gaw vehk*
Stop, thief!	**Stopp tyven!** *stohp <u>tui</u>´•vuhn*
Get a doctor!	**Hent en lege!**
	hehnt ehn <u>leh</u>`•guh

YOU MAY HEAR...

Kan du fylle ut dette skjemaet? *kahn dew <u>fui</u>`•luh ewt <u>deht</u>`•tuh <u>sheh</u>´•mah•uh*

Can you fill out this form?

ID, takk.
ee•deh tahk

Your ID, please.

Fire!	**Brann!** *brahn*
I'm lost.	**Jeg har gått meg bort.**
	*yay h**ah**r goht may boort*
Can you help me?	**Kan du hjelpe meg?**
	*kahn d**ew** <u>yehl</u>`•puh may*
Call the police!	**Ring politiet!** *ring pu•lih•<u>**tee**</u>´•uh*
Where's the police station?	**Hvor er politistasjonen?**
	*voor **ar** pu•lih•<u>**tee**</u>´•stah•sh**oo**•nuhn*
My child is missing.	**Barnet mitt er kommet bort.**
	<u>b**ahr**</u>`•nuh miht **ar** <u>kohm</u>`•muht boort*

In an emergency, dial: **112** for the police.
110 for the fire brigade
113 for medical emergencies.

Health

I'm sick [ill].	**Jeg er syk.** *yay ar suik*
I need an English-speaking doctor.	**Jeg trenger en lege som snakker engelsk.** *yay trehng´·uhr ehn <u>leh</u>`·guh sohm <u>snahk</u>`·kuhr <u>ehng</u>´·ehlsk*
It hurts here.	**Det gjør vondt her.** *deh yurr vunt har*
Where's the nearest pharmacy [chemist's]?	**Hvor er nærmeste apotek?** *voor ar <u>ner</u>`·mehs·tuh ah·pu·<u>teh</u>´k*
I'm ...months pregnant.	**Jeg er ...måneder gravid** *yay ar mawn·ehd·ehr grah·veed*
I'm on...	**Jeg går på...** *yay gawr poh...*
I'm allergic to antibiotics/penicillin.	**Jeg er allergisk mot antibiotika/penicillin.** *yay ar ah·<u>ler</u>´·gihsk moot ahn·tih·bih·<u>oo</u>´·tih·kah/ peh·nih·sih·<u>lee</u>n´*

Dictionary

A

a (common nouns) en; **(neuter nouns)** et
acetaminophen [paracetamol] paracetamol
adapter adapter
American *adj* amerikansk; *n* amerikaner
antiseptic cream antiseptisk salve
arthritis leddgikt
aspirin aspirin
asthma astma
at ved
ATM minibank

B

baby baby
baby bottle tåteflaske
baby wipes papirkluter
babysitter barnevakt
back *adv* **(direction)** tilbake;
  n **(body part)** rygg
backpack ryggsekk
bag (carrier) bærepose
baby baby
Band-Aid [plaster] plaster
bandage bandasje
beige beige
bikini bikini
black svart
bland smakløs
blue blå

bottle opener flaskeåpner
bowl (container) bolle
boy gutt
boyfriend kjæreste
bra behå
brown brun

C

cafe kafé
call *n* **(phone)** samtale;
  v **(phone)** ringe
camera kamera
can opener boksåpner
castle slott
cigarette sigarett
cold *adj* kald; *n* **(illness)** forkjølelse
comb kam
computer datamaskin
condom kondom
contact lens solution kontaktlinsevæske
corkscrew korketrekker
cup kopp

D

dairy melkeprodukter
damage *v* skade
dance *v* danse
dance club diskotek
dark mørk
day dag
deaf døv
deodorant deodorant

diabetic diabetiker
dog hund
doll dukke

E

earache øreverk
earring ørering
east øst
easy lett
eat *v* spise
economy class turistklasse
electrical outlet strømuttak
elevator heis
e-mail *n* **(message)** e-post; *v* sende e-post

F

face ansikt
facial ansiktsbehandling
family familie
fan (appliance) vifte
far langt
fork gaffel

G

game (match) kamp
garbage bag søppelsekk
garden hage
gas (car) bensin
gas station bensinstasjon
girl jente
girlfriend kjæreste
glass (drinking) glass
glasses (optical) briller

good god
gray grå
green grønn

H

hair hår
hair salon frisørsalong
hairbrush hårbørste
haircut klipp
hairdresser frisør
horse hest
hot varm
husband ektemann

I

I jeg
ibuprofen ibuprofen
ice is
icy kaldt
identification legitimasjon
ill [BE] syk
important viktig
in i
I'd like… Jeg vil gjerne…
insect repellent insektmiddel

J

jacket jakke
jeans olabukse
jewelry smykker

K

keep v beholde

key nøkkel
key card nøkkelkort
kiddie pool plaskebasseng
kiss v kysse
knife kniv

L

lactose intolerant laktoseintolerant
large stor
lighter lighter
love v elske

M

machine maskin
machine washable maskinvaskbar
magazine blad
magnificent storslagen
mail post
match (matchstick) fyrstikk; **(sport)** kamp
medium mellomstor
museum museum

N

nail (human) negl
nail file neglefil
nail salon neglesalong
name navn
napkin serviett
nurse sykepleier

O

off av
off-licence [BE] vinmonopol

office kontor
old gammel
on på
orange oransje

P

p.m. (afternoon) om ettermiddagen; **(evening)** om kvelden
pacifier (baby's) narresmokk
pack v pakke
package pakke
paddling pool [BE] plaskebasseng
pain smerte
park n park; v parkere
pen penn
pharmacy apotek
phone telefon
pink rosa
plate tallerken; **(dessert)** asjett
purple fiolett
pyjamas pyjamas

Q

question spørsmål
quick rask
quickly øyeblikkelig
quiet rolig

R

racecourse [BE] travbane
racetrack travbane
racket (sport) racket
railway station [BE] jernbanestasjon
rain n regn; v regne

raincoat regnfrakk

razor/disposable razor en barberhøvel/engangshøvel

razor blade barberblad

red rød

reservation bestilling

reserve *v* bestille

restaurant restaurant

restroom toalett

S

safe *adj* **(free from danger)** trygg; *n* safe

sandals sandaler

sanitary napkin sanitetsbind

saucer skål

sauna badstue

save (computer) lagre

scarf skjerf

salty salt

sandals sandaler

sanitary napkin sanitetsbind

sauna badstue

scissors saks

shampoo/conditioner sjampo/hårbalsam

shoes sko

single (unmarried) ugift

single ticket [BE] enveisbillett

size (clothes) størrelse; **(shoes)** nummer

small liten

sneakers turnsko

snow *n* snø; *v* snø

soap såpe

sock sokk

spicy krydret
spoon skje
stamp v stemple; n **(postage)** frimerke
suitcase koffert
sun sol
sunglasses solbriller
sunscreen solkrem
sweater genser
swimsuit badedrakt

T

table bord
tablet (medical) tablett
take v ta
tampon tampong
taste v smake
tax skatt
taxi drosje
taxi stand drosjeholdeplass
team lag
terrible forferdelig
tissue papirlommetørkle
toilet paper toalettpapir
toothbrush tannbørste
toothpaste tannpasta
tough seigt
toy leketøy
T-shirt T-skjorte

U

ugly stygg
umbrella paraply

until til
upset stomach urolig mage
use *n* bruk; *v* bruke
username brukernavn

V

vacation ferie
vegan veganer
vegetarian vegetarianer

W

wait *v* vente
waiter/waitress servitør
white hvit
wife kone
with med; **without** uten

Y

year år
yellow gul
yes ja
yesterday i går

Z

zoo dyrehage

Finnish

Essentials

Hello!	**Hei!** *hay*
Goodbye.	**Hyvästi.** *hew-vaes-ti*
Yes.	**Kyllä.** *kewl-lae*
No.	**Et.** *ayt*
OK.	**Hyväksyntä.** *hew-vaek-sewn-tah*
Excuse me! (to get attention, to get past)	**Anteeksi?** *ahn-tayk-si*
Sorry!	**Anteeksi!** *ahn-tayk-si*
I'd like...	**Haluaisin...** *Hah-loo-ice-in...*
How much?	**Paljonko maksaa?** *pahl-yon-koa muck-sah*
And/Or	**Ja/Tai** *yah/tie*
Where is...?	**Missä on...?** *miss-sah on...*
Please.	**Kiitos.** *kcy toss*
Thank you.	**Kiitos.** *key-toss*
You're welcome.	**Ei kestä.** *ay kes-tah*
I'm going to...	**Olen matkalla...-n/...-lle.** *oa-len mut-kul-lah...n/lle*
My name is...	**Nimeni on...** *ne-meh-ne on...*
Can you speak more slowly?	**Voitteko puhua hitaammin?** *voyt-te-koa poo-hoo-a hit-taam-min*
Can you repeat that?	**Voitteko toistaa?** *voyt-te-koa toais-taa*
I don't understand.	**En ymmärrä.** *ayn ewm-maer-ra*
Do you speak English?	**Puhutteko englantia?** *poo-hoot-tay-koa ayng-lahn-tiah*
I don't speak (much) Finnish.	**En puhu (paljoakaan) suomea.** *en poo-hoo (pahl-yoa-kaan) soomea*

171

Where is the restroom **Missä on WC?** *miss-sah on veh-se*
[toilet]?
Help!   **Apua!** *uh-po-uh*

Numbers

0	**nolla**	*knoll-uh*
1	**yksi**	*ewk-se*
2	**kaksi**	*kuk-se*
3	**kolme**	*col-meh*
4	**neljä**	*nell-yah*
5	**viisi**	*vee-se*
6	**kuusi**	*coo-se*
7	**seitsemän**	*sayt-seh-man*
8	**kahdeksan**	*kuh-deck-sun*
9	**yhdeksän**	*ewh-deck-san*
10	**kymmenen**	*kewm-meh-nan*
11	**yksitoista**	*ewk-se-toys-tuh*
12	**kaksitoista**	*kuk-se-toys-tuh*
13	**kolmetoista**	*col-meh-toys-tuh*
14	**neljätoista**	*nell-yah-toys-tuh*
15	**viisitoista**	*vee-se-toys-tuh*

You'll find the pronunciation of the Finnish letters and
words written in gray after each sentence to guide you. Simply
pronounce these as if they were English, noting that any underlines
and bolds indicate an additional emphasis or stress or a lengthening of
a vowel sound. As you hear the language being spoken, you will quickly
become accustomed to the local pronunciation and dialect.

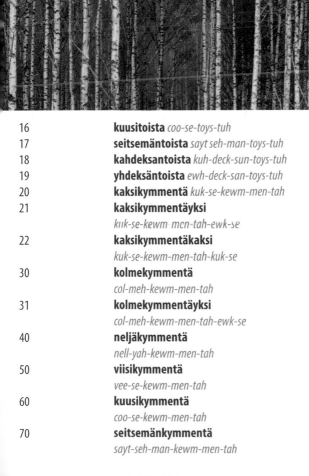

80	**kahdeksankymmentä**	
	kuh-deck-sun-kewm-men-tah	
90	**yhdeksänkymmentä**	
	ewh-deck-san-kewm-men-tah	
100	**sata** *su-tuh*	
101	**satayksi** *su-tuh-ewk-se*	
200	**kaksisataa** *kuk-se-su-tar*	
500	**viisisataa** *vee-se-su-tar*	
1,000	**tuhat** *too-hut*	
10,000	**kymmenen tuhatta**	
	kewm-men-nan too-hut-uh	
1,000,000	**miljoona** *mil-yawn-uh*	

Time

What time is it?	**Paljonko kello on?** *pul-yon-koh kell-lo on*
It's midday.	**On keskipäivä.** *on kes-ke-paey-vah*
Five past three.	**Viisi yli kolme.** *vee-se ew-le col-meh*
A quarter to ten.	**Varttia vaille kymmenen.**
	vurt-te-uh viel-leh kewm-men-nan
5:30 a.m./p.m.	**5.30/17.30** *vee-se col-meh-kewm-men-tah/sayt-seh-*
	man-toys-tuh col-meh-kewm-men-tah

Days

Monday	**Maanantai** *muh-nun-tie*
Tuesday	**Tiistai** *tease-tie*
Wednesday	**Keskiviikko** *kes-ke-veak-koh*
Thursday	**Torstai** *tors-tie*
Friday	**Perjantai** *per-yan-tie*
Saturday	**Lauantai** *lao un-tie*
Sunday	**Sunnuntai** *son-un-tie*

Dates

yesterday	**eilen** *ey-len*
today	**tänään** *tah-naan*
tomorrow	**huomenna** *huo-men-nuh*
day	**päivä** *paey-vah*
week	**viikko** *veak-koh*
month	**kuukausi** *coo-cow-se*
year	**vuosi** *vu-o-se*
Happy New Year!	**Hyvää uutta vuotta!**
	hew-ah oot-tuh vu-ot-tuh
Happy Birthday!	**Hyvää syntymäpäivää!**
	hew-ah s-ewn-tew-ma-paey-vah

Months

January	**Tammikuu** *tum-me-coo*
February	**Helmikuu** *hel-me-coo*
March	**Maaliskuu** *muh-lis-coo*
April	**Huhtikuu** *hooh-te-coo*
May	**Toukokuu** *to-o-koh-coo*
June	**Kesäkuu** *ke-sah-coo*
July	**Heinäkuu** *hey-nah-coo*
August	**Elokuu** *e-lo-coo*
September	**Syyskuu** *s-ews-coo*
October	**Lokakuu** *lo-ku-coo*
November	**Marraskuu** *mur-rus-coo*
December	**Joulukuu** *yo-lo-coo*

Arrival & Departure

I'm here on vacation [holiday]/business.	**Olen lomamatkalla/työmatkalla.** *oa-len lo-mu-mut-kul-lah/tew-mut-kul-lah*
I'm going to…	**Olen matkalla…-n/…-lle.** *oa-len mut-kul-lah…n/lle*
I'm staying at the…Hotel.	**Yövyn …hotellissa.** *ew-vynn…hot-ell-is-sah*

Money

Where's…?	**Missä on…?** *mis-sah on…*
the ATM	**pankkiautomaatti** *pung-kih-ow-toh-mut-te*
the bank	**pankki** *pung-kih*
the currency exchange office	**valuutanvaihtopiste** *vah-loot-un-vieh-toh-piss-teh*

What time does the bank open/close?	**Mihin aikaan pankki avautuu/sulkeutuu?** *me-hin ay-kaln pung-kih ah-vov-two/sol-keo-two*
I'd like to change some dollars/pounds into euros.	**Haluaisin vaihtaa dollareita/puntia euroiksi.** *hu-loh-ice-in vieh-tar dol-la-ray-tah/pon-te-ah eo-royk-se*

When using ATMs in Finland, you will notice that there is no distinction made between different types of account. However, it may be useful to know the correct Finnish terminology: a checking [current] account is **käyttötililtä** and a savings account is **säästötililtä**.

177

YOU MAY SEE...

The official currency in Finland is the **euro** (**€**), divided into 100 **cents**.
Coins: 1, 2, 5, 10, 20, 50 cents; €1, 2
Bills: €5, 10, 20, 50, 100, 200, 500

I want to cash some traveler's checks [cheques].	**Haluaisin lunastaa matkašekkejä.** *hu-loh-ice-in lo-nus-tar mut-ku-shake-a-yah*
Can I pay in cash?	**Voinko maksaa käteisellä ?** *voyn-koh muck-sar kah-tay-sel-lah*
Can I pay by credit card?	**Voinko maksaa luottokortilla?** *voyn-koh muck-sar lo-oh-toh-kor-til-lah*

For Numbers, see page 172.

Getting Around

How do I get to town?	**Miten pääsen kaupunkiin?** *mitt-ten paa-sen cow-pon-keen*
Where's...?	**Missä on...?** *mis-sah on...*
the airport	**lentoasema** *len-toh-uh-se-mu*
the train station	**juna-asema** *yu-nuh-uh-se-mu*
the bus station	**linja-autoasema** *lin-ya-ow-toh-uh-se-mu*
the subway station [underground]	**metroasema** *met-ro-uh-se-mu*

Public transport in Helsinki is operated by **Helsinki City Transport (HKL)**, **www.hel.fi/hkl**. Online you can find timetables, a journey planner and other useful information in English. There are a variety of ticket schemes available.

Is it far from here?	**Onko se kaukana täältä?**	
	ong-kohh seh cow-ku-nu tael-tah	
Where do I buy a ticket?	**Mistä ostan lipun?**	
	miss-tah oes-tun le-pon	
A one-way/return-trip ticket to...	**Menolippu/menopaluulippu ...-n/...-lle**	
	meh-noh-lip-poh/meh-noh-pu-loo-lip-poh...-n/-lle	
How much?	**Paljonko?** *pul-yon-ko*	
Which gate/line?	**Mikä portti/linja?**	
	me-kah port-te/lin-ya	
Which platform?	**Mikä laituri?**	
	me-kah lie-tu-re	
Where can I get a taxi?	**Mistä saan taksin?**	
	miss-tah suun tuk-sin	
Take me to this address.	**Viekää minut tähän osoitteeseen.**	
	vee-e-kah me-noot ta-han oa-soyt-teh-sen	

179

Boats are a popular mode of transport in Finland thanks to the country's many waterways and islands. Ferry travel between Sweden, Estonia and Germany is relatively simple, with many companies offering high-speed links. It is worth noting however that the Gulf of Finland freezes in the winter meaning some services are seasonal only.

To...Airport, please.	**... lentoasemalle, kiitos.**
	...len-toh-uh-se-mul-leh, key-toss
I'm in a rush.	**Minulla on kiire.** *me-noll-lah on key-reh*
Can I have a map?	**Saisinko kartan?**
	s-ay-sin-koh kar-tun

Tickets

When's...to Helsinki?	**Milloin menee... Helsinkiin?**
	mil-loin meh-neh... Hel-see-keen
the (first) bus	**(ensimmäinen) linja-auto**
	(en-sim-may-nan) lin-ya-ow-toh
the (next) flight	**(seuraava) lento** *(sew-ruu-vuh) len-toh*
the (last) train	**(viimeinen) juna** *(vee-may-nen) yu-nuh*
One/Two ticket(s)	**Yksi/Kaksi lippu(a), kiitos.**
please.	*ewk-se/kak-se lip-po-ah*
For today/tomorrow.	**Tälle päivälle/huomiselle.**
	täl-leh paey-val-leh/huo-me-sel-leh
A...ticket.	**...lippu.** *...lip-poh*
one-way	**Meno** *meh-noh*
return trip [return]	**Menopaluu** *meh-noh-pu-loo*
first class	**Ensimmäisen luokan** *en-sim-may-sen lo-oh-kun*

I have an e-ticket.	**Minulla on e-lippu.**	
	me-noll-la on ay-lip-poh	
How long is the trip?	**Kuinka pitkä matka on?**	
	coo-en-ku pit-kah mut-ku on	
Is it a direct train?	**Onko se suora junayhteys?**	
	ong-koh soo-o-ru yu-na-ewh-teh-ews	
Is this the bus to…?	**Onko tämä linja-auto…-n/…-lle?**	
	ong-koh ta-ma lin-ya-ow-toh…-n/…-lle	
Can you tell me when	**Voitteko kertoa minulle, missä jäädä pois?**	
to get off?	*voyt-teh-ku ker-toh-ah me-noll-leh,*	
	miss-sah yah-da poys	

Linja auto or coach is an important means of transportation in the northern regions as there are no railways. There are multiple companies in operation, each with their own timetables and prices so it is best to check at the local station. Services are frequent and while more expensive than train travel, they are comfortable and offer a speedy means of getting around.

Taxis are easy to spot as they all have a yellow **Taxi** or **Taksi** sign. If the sign is lit up, the taxi is available. All taxis are metered and a surcharge is applied at weekends and at nighttime. Tipping is appreciated.

YOU MAY HEAR...

suoraan eteenpäin *soo-o-rahn e-tehn-paeyn* — straight ahead
vasemmalle *vuh-sem-mul-leh* — left
oikealle *oi-ke-ul-leh* — right
kulman takana *kol-mun tuh-ku-nu* — around the corner
vastapäätä *vus-tuh-paa-tah* — opposite
takana *tu-ko-nu* — behind
vieressä *vee-e-res-sah* — next to
jälkeen *yal-ken* — after
pohjoinen/etelä *poh-yoi-nan/e-teh-lah* — north/south
itä/länsi *e-ta/lan-se* — east/west
liikennevaloissa *lea-ken-neh-vuh-loys-sah* — at the traffic light
risteyksessä *res-te-ew-k-ses-sah* — at the intersection

I'd like to...	**Haluaisin...** *hu-loh-ice-in...*
my reservation.	**varaukseni.** *vuh-ru-ok-se-ne*
cancel	**peruuttaa** *pey-root-tar*
change	**muuttaa** *moot-tar*
confirm	**vahvistaa** *vuh-vis-tar*

For Time, see page 174.

182

Car Hire

Where's the car hire?	**Missä on autovuokraamo?**
	miss-sah on ow-toh-vu-ok-ruu-moh
I'd like...	**Haluaisin...** *hul-oh-ice-in...*
a cheap/small car	**edullisen/pienen auton**
	e-dol-le-sen/pi-e-nan ow-ton
an automatic/ a manual	**automaattisen/manuaalisen vaihtelston**
	ow-toh-mut-te-sen/mu-noo-ah-le-sen vieh-tay-ton
air conditioning	**ilmastoinnin** *il-mus-toien-nen*
a car seat	**turvaistuimen** *toor-vu-is-tooe-men*

Metered parking is in operation in most places and there will be clear signs to indicate this. Payment is usually in a machine located in the vicinity or through displaying a disc which can be purchased in a local shop.

Essentials

How much…?	**Paljonko…?** *pul-yon-ko…*
per day/week	**päivää/viikkoa kohti**
	paey-vah/veak-koah koh-te
Are there any	**Annatteko alennuksia?**
discounts?	*un-nut-teh-ku uh-len-nook-se-uh*

Places to Stay

Can you recommend	**Voitteko suositella hotellia?**
a hotel?	*voyt-teh-ku soo-o-se-tel-lah hot-ell-ee-ah*
I made a reservation.	**Minulla on varaus.** *me-noll-ah on vuh-ru-os*
My name is…	**Nimeni on…** *ne-meh-ne on…*
Do you have a	**Onko teillä huonetta…?**
room…?	*ong-koh tail-la huo-net-tuh…*
for one/two	**yhdelle/kahdelle** *ewh-del-leh/kuh-del-leh*

The standard of Finnish **hotelli** is usually excellent. Most have saunas as well as swimming pools. The national tourist board has lots of information on places to stay and is a useful starting point for planning your journey, visit www.visitfinland.com.

Camping season starts at the end of May in the south and lasts into September. There are hundreds of campsites to choose from and more than 200 of these belong to the Finnish Travel Association, **Suomen Matkailuliitto**. Campsites are graded from one to three stars and the top sites offer activities such as horse riding, waterskiing, rowing and fishing. An international or Finnish camping card will be required – these can be obtained on site.

with a bathroom	**kylpyhuoneella** *kewl-pew-huo-nel-lah*
with air conditioning	**ilmastoinnilla** *il-mus-toyn-nil-lah*
For...	
tonight	**täksi illaksi** *tax-e il-luck-se*
two nights	**kahdeksi yöksi** *kuh-deck-se ewk-se*
one week	**yhdeksi viikoksi** *ewh-deck-se veak-ox-e*
How much?	**Paljonko?** *pul-yon-ko*
Is there anything cheaper?	**Onko mitään halvempaa?** *ong-koh me-taen hul-vem-puh*
When's checkout?	**Mihin aikaan uloskirjautuminen on?** *me-hin ay-kaln o-los-ker-yaow-tu-me-nan on*
Can I leave this in the safe?	**Voinko jättää tämän tallelokeroon?** *voyn-ku yat-tae ta-man tul-leh-lo-ke-rawn*

Local tourist offices are an excellent source for accommodation, activity and entertainment options; see **www.visitfinland.com** for more information.

Can I leave my bags?	**Voinko jättää laukkuni säilytykseen?**
	voyn-ku yat-tae laok-ko-ne sah-el-ewt-ewk-sen
Can I have my bill/	**Saisinko laskun/kuitin?**
a receipt?	*s-ay-sing-ku lus-kon/quit-in*
I'll pay in cash/	**Maksan käteisellä/luottokortilla.**
by credit card.	*muck-sun kah-tay-sel-lah/lo-oh-toh-skor-til-lah*

Communications

Where's an	**Missä on internet-kahvila?**
internet cafe?	*miss-sah on internet-kun-ve-luh*
Can I access the	**Voinko käyttää internetiä/tarkistaa**
internet/check my	**sähköpostini?** *voyn-ku kaot-tae*
email?	*internet-ew-a/tur-kiss-tar sah-koeh-pos-tinny*
How much per half	**Paljonko maksaa puoli tuntia/tunti?**
hour/hour?	*pul-yon-ko muck-sar poh-oe-le tunn-te-uh/tunn-te*
How do I connect/	**Miten muodostan yhteyden?**
log on?	*me-ten mo-oh-dos-tun ewh-te-ew-den*
A phone card, please.	**Puhelinkortti, kiitos.**
	poh-el-in-kort-te, key-toss

Can I have your	**Saanko puhelinnumerosi?**
phone number?	*suun-ku poh-el-in-noo-meh-ro-se*
Here's my	**Tässä on puhelinnumeroni/**
number/email.	**sähköpostiosoitteeni.**
	tas-sah on poh-el-in-noo-meh-ro-ne/
	sah-koeh-pos-te-oa-soyt-teh-ne
Call me.	**Soita minulle.** *soy-tuh me-noll-leh*
Text me.	**Lähetä minulle tekstiviesti.**
	la-he-tah me-noll-leh tex-te-vee-es-te
I'll text you.	**Lähetän sinulle tekstiviestin.**
	la-he-tan se-noll-leh tex-te-vee-es-tin

A symbolic hunting horn and the words **Posti-Post** identify
post offices in Finland. Mailboxes are painted yellow. Normal
business hours are Monday to Friday from 9:00 a.m. to 6:00 p.m.
A limited service also operates out of hours in the Helsinki railway
station from 7:00 a.m. to 9:00 p.m weekdays and from 10:00 a.m until
6:00 p.m on weekends.

Email me.	**Lähetä minulle sähköpostia.**	187
	la-he-tah me-noll-leh sah-koeh-pos-te-uh	
Hello. This is…	**Hei. Täällä on…** *hey, tael-lah on…*	
Can I speak to…?	**Onko…tavoitettavissa?**	
	ong-koh…tuh-voy-tet-tuh-vis-suh	
Can you repeat that?	**Voitteko toistaa?** *voyt-teh-ku toys-tar*	
I'll call back later.	**Soitan myöhemmin takaisin.**	
	soy-tun m-ew-hem-min tuck-ice-in	
Bye.	**Hei hei.** *hey hey*	
Where's the	**Missä on postitoimisto?**	
post office?	*miss-sah on pos-te-toy-mis-toh*	

I'd like to send this to...	**Haluaisin lähettää tämän...-n/...-lle.** *hul-oh-ice-in la-het-tae ta-man...-n/...-lle*
Can I...?	**Voinko...?** *voyn-ku...*
access the internet	**käyttää internetiä** *kaot-tae internet-ew-a*
check my email	**tarkistaa sähköpostini** *tur-kiss-tar sah-koeh-pos-tinny*
print	**tulostaa** *to-loss-tar*
plug in/charge my laptop/iPhone/ iPad/BlackBerry?	**ladata kannettavan tietokoneeni/iPhoneni/ iPadini/BlackBerryni?** *luh-du-tuh kun-net-tuh-vun te-e-toh-ku-neh-ne/iPhone-eh-ne/ iPad-e-ne/BlackBerry-ne*
access Skype?	**käyttää Skypeä?** *kaot-tae Skype-eh-a*
What is the WiFi password?	**Mikä langattoman verkon salasana on?** *me-kah lung-ah-toh-mun ver-kon su-lu-su-nu on*
Is the WiFi free?	**Onko langaton verkko maksuton?** *ong-koh lung-ah-ton verk-ku muck-su-on*
Do you have bluetooth?	**Onko teillä bluetooth-yhteyttä?** *ong-koh tail-la bluetooth-ewh-teh-ewt-tah*
Do you have a scanner?	**Onko teillä skanneria?** *ong-koh tail-la skun-neh-re-uh*

Social Media

Are you on Facebook/Twitter?	**Oletko Facebookissa/Twitterissä?** *oa-let-ku Facebook-is-suh/Twitter-is-sah*
What's your username?	**Mikä käyttäjänimesi on?** *me-kah kaot-ta-yah-ne-meh-se on*
I'll add you as a friend.	**Lisään sinut kaveriksi.** *le-saen se-noot ku-veh-rick-se*
I'll follow you on Twitter.	**Seuraan sinua Twitterissä.** *saw-raan se-noo-uh Twitter-is-sah*
Are you following…?	**Seuraatko…?** *sew-raat-ku…*
I'll put the pictures on Facebook/Twitter.	**Laitan kuvat Facebookiin/Twitteriin.** *lie-tun ko-vut Facebook-een/Twitter-een*
I'll tag you in the pictures.	**Merkitsen sinut kuviin.** *mer-kit-sen se-noot ko-veen*

189

Conversation

Hello./Hi!	**Hei!** *hay*
How are you?	**Mitä kuuluu?** *mit-ta koo-loo*
Fine, thanks.	**Kiitos hyvää.** *kee-toass hew-vae*
Excuse me!	**Anteeksi!** *ahn-tayk-si*

Finnish has two words for 'you' – the polite form **te** and the informal **sinä**. The polite form **te** is used as a mark of respect or when speaking to someone you do not know. **Sinä** is used among family and friends and with children. If in doubt as to which to use, always use the polite form.

Do you speak English?	**Puhutteko englantia?**
	poo-hoot-tay-koa ayng-lahn-tiah
What's your name?	**Mikä sinun nimesi on?**
	me-ka si-noon ni-may-si on
My name is...	**Minun nimeni on...**
	me-noon ni-may-ni on...
Nice to meet you.	**Hauska tavata.**
	house-kah tah-vah-tah
Where are you from?	**Mistä olet kotoisin?**
	miss-ta oa-let koa-toai-sin
I'm from the U.K./U.S.	**Olen kotoisin Isosta-Britanniasta/ Yhdysvalloista.** *oa-len koa-toai-sin I-soas-tah-Bri-tahn-neeah-stah/Ewh-dews-vahl-loai-stah*

The Northern Lights are a big draw to the country and the best place to see them is in northern Lapland in the Arctic Circle. During the dark winter months here, the sun rarely peaks its head over the horizon and you can expect to see the aurora borealis quite regularly. Other peak seasons include February and March and September through October.

What do you do for a living?	**Mitä teet työksesi?** *mit-tae tayt tew-urk-sa-si*
I work for…	**Olen töissä…** *oa-len tur-is-sae…*
I'm a student.	**Olen opiskelija.** *oa-len oa-pees-kee-li-yah*
I'm retired.	**Olen eläkkeellä.** *oa-len ay-lak-kayl-la*

Romance

Would you like to go out for a drink/dinner?	**Haluaisitko lähteä drinkille/syömään?** *ha-loo-ice-it-koa laeh-te-ah drin-keel-lay/sew-maen*
What are your plans for tonight/tomorrow?	**Mitä suunnitelmia sinulla on tänä iltana/huomenna?** *mee-ta soon-nee-tel-mee-ah si-nool-lah on tae-na il-tah-nah/hoa-mayn-nah*
Can I have your (phone) number?	**Saanko puhelinnumerosi?** *saan-koa poo-he-lin-noo-me-roa-si*
Can I join you?	**Voinko liittyä seuraasi?** *voyn-koa leet-tew-a say-oo-raa-si*
Can I buy you a drink?	**Voinko tarjota sinulle juotavaa?** *voyn-koa tar-joa-tah yo-tah-vaa*
I love you.	**Rakastan sinua.** *ra-kahs-tahn see-noo-ah*

Accepting & Rejecting

I'd love to.	**Mieluusti.** *mi-ay-loos-tee*
Where should we meet?	**Missä tapaisimme?** *miss-sae ta-pa-hi-sim-me*
I'll meet you at the bar/your hotel.	**Tavataan baarissa/hotellillasi.** *tah-vah-taan baa-ris-sah/hoa-tel-lil-la-see*
I'll come by at...	**Tulen kello...** *too-len kayl-loa...*
I'm busy.	**Olen kiireinen.** *oa-len kee-rayi-nen*
I'm not interested.	**En ole kiinnostunut.** *ayin oa-lay keen-noas-too-noot*
Leave me alone.	**Jätä minut rauhaan.** *ja-ta mi-noot rah-oo-haan*
Stop bothering me!	**Lakkaa häiritsemästä minua!** *lak-kaa haei-rit-se-mahs-tah mi-noo-ah*

Food & Drink

Eating Out

Can you recommend a good restaurant/ bar?	**Voitteko suositella hyvää ravintolaa/baaria?** *voyt-teh-ku soo-o-se-tel-lah hew-ah ru-ven-toh-luh/ baa-rea*
Is there a traditional/ an inexpensive restaurant nearby?	**Onko lähistöllä perinteistä/edullista ravintolaa?** *ong-koh la-his-tul-lah pey-ren-tase- tah/e-dol-lis-tuh ru-ven-toh-luh*
A table for…, please.	**Pöytä…:lle, kiitos.** *poe-tah….:lle, key-toss*
Can we sit…?	**Voimmeko istua…?** *voym-meh-koh is-too-uh…*
here/there	**tässä/tuolla** *tas-sah/two-ol-luh*
outside	**ulkona** *ol-koh-nuh*
in a non-smoking area	**savuttomalla alueella** *su-vol-toh-mul-luh uh-lo-el-luh*
I'm waiting for someone.	**Odotan seuraa.** *oa-do-tun sew-rah*
Where are the toilets?	**Missä on WC?** *miss-sah on veh-se*
The menu, please.	**Saisinko ruokalistan, kiitos.** *sigh-sing-koh roo-o-kuh-lis-tun, key-toss*
What do you recommend?	**Mitä suosittelette?** *me-tah soo-o-sit-teh-let-teh*
I'd like…	**Haluaisin…** *hal-oh-ice-in…*
Some more…, please.	**Lisää…, kiitos.** *le-sae… key-toss*
Enjoy your meal!	**Hyvää ruokahalua!***hew-ah roo-o-kuh-hu-loa*
The check [bill], please.	**Lasku, kiitos.** *lus-ko, key-toss*

YOU MAY SEE...

PALVELUMAKSU	cover charge
KIINTEÄ HINTA	fixed price
(PÄIVÄN) RUOKALISTA	menu (of the day)
PALVELU SISÄLTYY (EI SISÄLLY) HINTAAN	service (not) included
ERIKOISET	specials

Is service included? **Sisältyykö palvelumaksu hintaan?**
se-sal-two-koeh pul-veh-loh-muck-soo hin-taan

Can I pay by credit **Voinko maksaa luottokortilla/saada kuitin?**
card/have a receipt? *voyn-ko muck-sar lo-oh-toh-kor-til-lah/*
sar-duh quit-in

Mealtime in Finland is often earlier than in most other European countries. Lunch at 11:00 a.m is not unusual and dinner in the evening is usually eaten around 5:00 p.m. However, these times do not apply to restaurants, where food is served much later.

Breakfast

bacon	**pekoni** *pey-koh-ne*
bread	**leipä** *lay-pah*
butter	**voi** *voy*
cold cuts	**leikkeleet** *layk-ke-leht*
cheese	**juusto** *yoos-toh*

...egg	**...muna** ...*mo-nuh*
hard/soft-boiled	**kovaksi/pehmeäksi keitetty**
	koh-vack-se/payh-meh-ack-se kay-tet-tew
fried	**paistettu** *pies-tet-tew*
scrambled	**munakokkeli** *mo-nuh-kock-ke-le*
jam/jelly	**hillo** *hill-oh*
omelet	**munakas** *mo-nuh-cuss*
toast	**paahtoleipä** *puh-toh-lay-pah*
sausage	**makkara** *muck-ku-ruh*
yogurt	**jogurtti** *yu-gort-te*

Finland has its own version of the Swedish smörgåsbord called **Seisova pöytä**. It can work as either a first course only or as a fixed-price buffet and often consists of more than 50 dishes. The meal is usually divided into three phases, starting with fish, then cold meats and ending with hot dishes such as meatballs and casseroles. There will also be a selection of salads, cheese, fruit bread, drinks and beer.

Appetizers

pasteija *pass-tay-yah*	pâté
kalakeitto *kahlah-kate-toh*	fish soup
vihaneskeitto *vihahnnays-kate-toh*	vegetable soup
tomaattikeitto *toh-mut-teh-kate-toh*	tomato soup
kanakeitto *kahnah-kate-toh*	chicken soup
leikkeleet *layk-ke-leht*	coldcuts
salaatti *su-lart-eh*	salad
savusilakoita *savoo-sill-le*	smoked herring
kaali-puolukkasalaatti *car-le-pooh-look-kuh-su-lart-eh*	cabbage and lingonberry salad

Smoked fish is somewhat of a speciality in Finland and you will find many fish dishes on the menu. It may also be grilled, glow-fired, steamed or basted in the oven. Salmon soup is another delicacy, as is **graavi lohi** (raw salmon marinated for a day in salt and herbs. **Graavi** is the Finnish version of sushi, served with small potatoes and dill in lieu of rice and seaweed.

YOU MAY HEAR...

puolikypsä *poh-oe-le-kewp-sae* — rare
keskikypsä *kes-ke-kewp-sae* — medium
hyvin/kypsäksi paistettu — well-done
hewvin/kewp-saeksi pies-tet-tew

Meat

naudanliha *now-dun-le-hah* — beef
hirvenliha *hir-ven-le-huh* — elk/moose
kana *ku-nuh* — chicken
lammas *lum-mus* — lamb
sianliha *syan-le-huh* — pork
pihvi *peah-ve* — steak
poronlihaa *poaroanleehah* — reindeer meat
vasikanliha *vuh-sick-un-le-huh* — veal

Fish & Seafood

turska *toors-kuh*	cod
kolja *col-yah*	haddock
kalmari *kul-muh-re*	squid
kampasimpukat *come-puh-sim-poh-cut*	scallops
silli *sill-le*	herring
hummeri *hom-meh-re*	lobster
lohi *loh-ee*	salmon
katkarapu *cut-kuh-ruh-puh*	shrimp/prawn

Vegetables

pavut *puh-voot*	beans
kaali *car-le*	cabbage
porkkana *porc-kuh-nuh*	carrot

Berries grow everywhere in Finland and cloudberries (**lakka**),
blueberries (**mustikka**) and lingonberries (**puolukka**) can be
found in everything from desserts to fruit teas and liqueurs.

Cheese is most often eaten at breakfast, thinly sliced, or alongside main courses in Finland rather than after dinner as is popular in other countries.

sieni *sye-neh*	mushroom
sipuli *se-poh-le*	onion
herneet *her-net*	peas
peruna *pay-roo-nuh*	potato
tomaatti *toh-mut-teh*	tomato

Measurements in Europe are metric, and that applies to the weight of food too. If you tend to think in pounds and ounces, it's worth brushing up on what the metric equivalent is before you go shopping for fruit and veg in markets and supermarkets. Five hundred grams, or half a kilo, is a common quantity to order, and that converts to just over a pound (17.65 ounces, to be precise).

Sauces & Condiments

Salt	**Suola** *soo-o-luh*
Pepper	**Pippuri** *pip-poh-re*
Mustard	**Sinappi** *se-nup-pe*
Ketchup	**Ketsuppi** *ket-sop-pe*

Fruit & Dessert

omena *oh-meh-nu*	apple
banaani *ba-nuh-ne*	banana
sitruuna *sit-roo-nuh*	lemon
appelsiini *up-pel-see-ne*	orange
päärynä *paa-rew-nah*	pear
mansikka *mun-sick-kah*	strawberry
jäätelö *yah-teh-loe*	ice cream
suklaa *sook-luh*	chocolate
vanilja *vuh-nil-yah*	vanilla
torttu *toarttoo*	tart
kakku *kuck-kuh*	cake
vaniljakastike *vuh-nil-yah-cuss-te-keh*	custard
kerma *ker-muh*	cream

Finland is a nation of coffee drinkers and it is common to invite people over for coffee rather than dinner. At mealtimes however, milk or buttermilk is the drink of choice, or else water or beer.

Drinks

The wine list/drink menu, please.	**Saisinko viinilistan/juomalistan, kiitos.** *sigh-sing-koh vee-ne-lis-tun/* *yuo-muh-lis-tun, key-toss*
What do you recommend?	**Mitä suosittelette?** *me-tah soo-o-sit-teh-let-teh*
I'd like a bottle/glass of red/white wine.	**Haluaisin pullon/lasin punaviiniä/valkoviiniä.** *hal-oh-ice-in pull-on/luh-sin po-nuh-vee-near/* *vul-koh-vee-near*
The house wine, please.	**Talon viiniä, kiitos.** *tuh-lon vee-near, key-toss*
Another bottle/glass, please.	**Toinen pullo/lasi, kiitos.** *toy-nan pull-loh/luh-se, key-toss*
I'd like a local beer.	**Haluaisin paikallista olutta.** *hal-oh-ice-in pie-kal-lis-tuh oa-loot-uh*

Can I buy you a drink?	**Voinko ostaa sinulle juotavaa?**
	voyn-koh oes-tuh se-noll-eh yuo-tuh-var
Cheers!	**Kippis!** *kip-piss*
A coffee/tea, please.	**Kahvi/tee, kiitos.**
	kuh-veh/teh, key-toss
Black.	**Mustana** *mos-tu-nuh*
With...	**kanssa** *kahnssah*
milk	**maidolla** *my-dol-uh*
sugar	**sokerilla** *so-ke-rel-luh*
artificial	**makeutusaineella**
sweetener	*mu-keo-tos-ay-nal-luh*
A..., please.	**..., kiitos.** *... key-toss*
juice	**tuoremehu** *two-o-reh-ma-ho*
soda	**limsa** *lem-suh*
(sparkling/still)	**(hiilihapollinen/hiilihapoton) vesi**
water	*(hee-le-hu-pol-le-nan/hee-le-hu-po-ton) veh-se*

The minimum legal age for drinking is 18 in Finland. Alcohol is generally more expensive than in the UK and US and beer, vodka and liqueurs are the most popular alcohol beverages. A popular liqueur made from cloudberries is **Lapponia Lakka**, while at Christmas **glögi** is a popular hot, spiced red wine and berry drink. The most popular beer in Finland is **Lapin Kulta** (Lapland's Gold). It is brewed with water from clear mountain streams in northern Lapland. Wine is expensive but both imported and local varieties can be found.

Leisure Time

Sightseeing

Where's the tourist information office?	**Missä on matkailuneuvonta?** *miss-sae on maht-kaye-loo-nay-von-tah*
What are the main sights?	**Mitkä ovat tärkeimmät nähtävyydet?** *met-ka oa-vaht tar-kaym-mat nah-ta-vew-det*
Do you offer tours in English?	**Onko teillä englanninkielisiä kierroksia?** *oan-ko tayl-la ayng-lahn-nin-ki-ay-li-si-ae ki-er-rock-si-ah*
Can I have a map/guide?	**Saisinko kartan/oppaan?** *sahi-sin-koa kahr-tahn/oap-paan*

Shopping

Where's the market/mall?	**Missä on tori/ostoskeskus?** *miss-sae on toa-ri/oas-toas-kesh-koos*

YOU MAY SEE...

AVOINNA/KIINNI	open/closed
SISÄÄNKÄYNTI/ULOS	entrance/exit

Stockmann's is a bit of an institution in Finland and it is the department store of choice for elusive and hard-to-find items or special gifts. There are branches throughout the country. It also owns **Akateeminen Kirjakauppa**, the country's best-known bookstore. Another department store worth visiting is **Sokos**, which has a great food hall.

I'm just looking.	**Katselen vain.** *kaht-sa-len vah-in*
Can you help me?	**Voitteko auttaa?**
	voyt-ta-koa ah-oot-taa
I'm being helped.	**Minua palvellaan.**
	mee-noo-ah pahl-val-laan
How much?	**Paljonko maksaa?**
	pahl-yon-koa muck-saa
That one, please.	**Tuo, kiitos.** *too-oa, kee-toas*
I'd like...	**Haluaisin...** *hul-oh-ice-in...*
That's all.	**Ei muuta.** *ayi moo-tah*
Where can I pay?	**Missä voin maksaa?**
	miss-sae voyn muck-saa

Typical souvenirs include objects made of wood, **puukko**
hunting knives and reindeer skins and antlers. Lapp crafts are
popular also; look for carvings made from reindeer bones, items
made from felt and traditional dolls.

I'll pay in cash/	**Maksan käteisellä/luottokortilla.**
by credit card.	*muck-sahn kae-tay-sal-lah/loo-oat-toa-kort-il-lah*
A receipt, please.	**Saisinko kuitin, kiitos.**
	sahi-sin-koa kooi-tin, kee-toas

Business hours in Finland require an early start - often 8:00
a.m., and lunch can be as early as 11:00 a.m., with 1:00 p.m.
being the outside limit. During the summer, many offices close at
3:00 p.m., or earlier, on Fridays.

Sport & Leisure

When's the game?	**Milloin peli alkaa?**
	meel-loa-in pe-li ahl-kaa
Where's...?	**Missä on...?** *miss-sah on...*
the beach	**ranta** *rahn-tah*
the park	**puisto** *poo-is-toa*
the pool	**uima-allas** *ooi mah ahl las*
Is it safe to swim here?	**Onko täällä turvallista uida?**
	oan-koa tael-lae toor-vahl-lis-tah ooi-da
Can I hire clubs?	**Voiko mailoja vuokrata?**
	voy-ko may-loa-ya voo-oak-rah-tah

Cross-country skiing is the most popular sport in Finland and most children learn to ski from the age of 3 or 4. The ski season runs from late October until the snow melts in May in Lapland and from January to March in the south of the country. Skating and ice hockey are other favorite winter sports.

The Finnish coast, combined with its vast network of inland waterways and lakes, means that boating, canoeing and kayaking are all popular pursuits. The waters can be enjoyed from any type of boat, from a one-man dinghy to a full-on sailing yacht or cruiser; most harbors have guest marinas.

How much per hour/day?	**Paljonko tunti/päivä maksaa?**
	pahl-yon-koa toon-ti/pae-i-vah muck-saa
How far is it to...?	**Kuinka kaukana on...?**
	kooin-kah cow-kah-nah on...
Show me on the map, please.	**Näyttäkää minulle kartalla, olkaa hyvä.**
	nayt-ta-kae mee-nol-la kahr-tahl-lah, oal-kaa hew-va

Going Out

What's there to do at night?	**Mitä tekemistä täällä on iltaisin?** *mi-tae te-ke-miss-tah tael-lah on il-tah-i-sin*
Do you have a program of events?	**Onko teillä tapahtumaohjelmaa?** *on-koa tayl-la tah-pah-too-mah-oah-yel-maa*
What's playing tonight?	**Mitä tänään tapahtuu?** *mi-ta ta naen tah-pah-too*
Where's...?	**Missä on...?** *miss-sae on...*
the downtown area	**keskusta** *kes-koos-tah*
the bar	**baari** *baa-ri*
the dance club	**yökerho** *er-ur-ker-hoa*
Is this area safe at night?	**Onko tämä alue turvallinen yöllä?** *on-koa ta-ma ah-loo-e toor-vahl-li-nen ew-url-la*

During the summer months, open air dances are very popular. These are held on large, purpose-built platforms called **tanssilava** and are usually situated in picturesque settings such as near a lake or in a forest clearing.

Baby Essentials

Do you have…?	**Onko teillä…?**	*on-koa tayl-la…*
a baby bottle	**tuttipulloa**	*toat-ti-pull-lo-ah*
baby food	**vauvanruokaa**	*wow-van-roo-oah-kaa*
baby wipes	**kosteuspyyhkeitä**	
	kos-tey-oos-pewh-kay-tah	
a car seat	**turvaistuinta**	*toor-vah-is-too-in-tah*
a children's menu/portion	**lasten ruokalistaa/annosta**	
	lahs-ten roo-oa-kah-lis-taa/ahn-noas-tah	

Finland is generally very safe and child-friendly. It is also home to child-friendly attractions such as Moominworld (www.muumimaailma.fi), a theme park in the south west of the country, and the Santa Claus Village (www.santaclausvillage.info) in Rovaniemi, straddling the Artic Circle up north. Public transport is also geared for use by parents with young children and prams, and getting around with children may be easier than in almost any other country.

a child's seat/	**lasten tuolia/syöttötuolia**
highchair	*lahs-ten tooa-li-ah/sewt-tur-tooa-li-ah*
a crib/cot	**vauvansänkyä/lasten sänkyä**
	wow-ahn-saen-kew-ae/lahs-ten saen-kew-ae
diapers [nappies]	**vaippoja** *vaye-ppoa-jah*
formula	**äidinmaidonkorviketta**
	aei-din-mayc don-koar-vi-kel-luh
a pacifier [dummy]	**tuttia** *toot-ti-ah*
a playpen	**leikkikehää** *layk-ki-ke-hae*
a stroller	**rattaita**
[pushchair]	*raht-taye-tah*
Can I breastfeed	**Voinko imettää täällä?**
the baby here?	*voyn-koa i-mayt-tae tael-la*
Where can I	**Missä voin imettää/vaihtaa vauvan vaipan?**
breastfeed/change	*miss-sa voyn i-mayt-tae wow-ahn*
the baby?	

Disabled Travelers

Is there...?	**Onko siellä...?** *on-koa si-ayl-lae...*
access for	**esteetön pääsy liikuntaesteisille**
the disabled	*ays-tay-toan pae-sew lee-koon-tah-ays-tayi-sil-le*
a wheelchair ramp	**pyörätuoliluiska** *pew-ra-toa-oo-li-loois-kah*
a disabled-	**invalidi-WC** *in-vah-li-di-vee-se*
accessible toilet	
I need...	**Tarvitsen...** *tar-vit-sen...*
assistance	**apua** *ah-poo-ah*
an elevator [a lift]	**hissin** *his-sin*
a ground-floor	**ensimmäisen kerroksen huoneen**
room	*ayn-sin-maei-sen ker-roak-sen hooa-nayn*
Please speak louder.	**Puhukaa kovempaa, olkaa hyvä.**
	poo-hoo-kaa koa-vem-paa, oal-kaa hew-vae

In an emergency, dial 112.
For maritime rescue services, call 0204100.

Health & Emergencies

Emergencies

Help!	**Apua!** *uh-po-uh*
Go away!	**Mene pois!** *meh-neh poys*
Stop, thief!	**Seis, varas!** *says, vuh-rus*
Get a doctor!	**Hakekaa lääkäri!** *hu-ke-car lae-kah-re*
Fire!	**Tuli on irti!** *tool-e on er-te*
I'm lost.	**Olen eksynyt.** *oa-len eck-s-ew-newt*

YOU MAY HEAR...

Täyttäkää tämä lomake.
tae-ewt-ta-kah tah-ma lo-mu-ke

Fill out this form.

Henkilöllisyystodistuksenne, olkaa hyvä.
*hen-ke-loel-le-s-ews-toh-dis-took-sen-neh,
oal-car hew-vah*

Your ID, please.

Milloin/missä tämä tapahtui?
mil-loin/miss-sah tah-ma tuh-puh-tooe

When/Where did it happen?

Miltä hän näyttää?
mil-tah han nawt-tae

What does he/she look like?

Can you help me?	**Voitteko auttaa minua?**
	voyt-teh-koh owt-tar me-noo-uh
Call the police!	**Soittakaa poliisit!** *soyt-tuh-car pol-ease-it*
Where's the	**Missä on poliisiasema?**
police station?	*miss-sah on pol-ease-e-uh-se-mu*
My child is missing.	**Lapseni on kadonnut.** *lup-seh-ne on ku-don-noot*

Health

I'm sick.	**Olen sairas.** *oa-len sigh-rus*
I need an English-	**Tarvitsen lääkärin, joka puhuu englantia.**
speaking doctor.	*tur-vit-sen lae-kah-ren, yo-ku po-hoo ang-lun-te-uh*
It hurts here.	**Tähän sattuu.** *ta-han sut-too*
Where's the	**Missä on apteekki?**
pharmacy?	*miss-sah on up-tehk-ke*
I'm (...months)	**Olen (...kuulla) raskaana.**
pregnant.	*oa-len (...cool-luh) rus-car-nuh*
I'm on...	**Käytän...** *kao-tan...*
I'm allergic to	**Olen allerginen antibiooteille/penisilliinille.**
antibiotics/penicillin.	*oa-len ul-ler-gy-nen un-teh-be-awe-tail-leh*
	pen-izzy-lean-il-leh

Dictionary

A

a (with nouns) (articles do not exist in Finnish)
adapter sovitin
address *n* osoite
American amerikkalainen
and ja
antiseptic cream antiseptinen voide
aspirin aspiriini

B

baby vauva
backpack reppu
bad huono, kehno
bag (purse/[handbag]); (shopping) laukku; kassi
Band-Aid [plasters] laastareita
bandage *n* side
battleground taistelukenttä
beige beige
bikini bikini
bird lintu
black musta
bland mautonta
blue sininen
bottle opener pullonavaaja
bowl kulho
boy poika
boyfriend poikaystävä
bra rintaliivit
British (person) britti
brown ruskea

C

cabin (ship) hytti
cafe kahvila
camera kamera
can opener tölkinavaaja
castle slot; linna
cigarette savuke
cold (illness) ; *adj* vilustuminen; kylmä
comb kampa
computer (PC) tietokone
condom kondomi
contact lens solution piilolinssinestettä
corkscrew korkkiruuvi
cup kuppi

D

dairy meijeri
damaged vaurioitunut
dangerous vaarallinen
deodorant deodorantti
diabetic diabeetikko
dog koira
doll nukke

E

each joka
ear korva
ear drops korvatipat
earache korvasärky
early aikainen, aikaisin
earring korvakoru
east itä

easy helppo
eat syödä
e-mail sähköposti
eye silmä

F

fabric (cloth) kangas
face kasvot
ferry lautta
fork haarukka
fresh tuore **(of food)**, raikas **(of air and water)**
friend ystävä
from suunnasta
frost pakkanen

G

gallery galleria
game peli
garage autotalli, korjaamo
garbage roska
girl tyttö
girlfriend tyttöystävä
glass (drinking) lasi
glasses (optical) silmälasit
good hyvä
gray harmaa
great (excellent) hieno
green vihreä

217

H

hair hiukset
hair dryer hiustenkuivain
hairbrush hiusharja

haircut tukanleikkuu
hairdresser kampaaja
hot (temperature) kuuma
husband aviomies
husband aviomies

I

I minä
ice jää
icy (weather) jäinen
identification (card) henkilöllisyystodistus
if jos
injection ruiske
I'd like… Haluaisin…
insect repellent hyönteismyrkky
Irish (person); *adj* irlantilainen

J

jacket jakku
jeans farkut

K

keep pitää
key avain
key card avainkortti
kiddie pool lastenallas
kind *adj ; n* ystävällinen; laatu
kiss *v* suudella
knife veitsi

L

lactose intolerant laktoosi-intolerantikko
large suuri
license (driving) ajokortti

life boat pelastusvene
lighter sytytin **(tool used to produce a flame)**; vaaleampi **(color)**;
  kevyempi **(weight)**
lotion kosteusemulsio
love v rakastaa

M

magazine aikakauslehti
magnificent suurenmoinen
mail *n ; v* posti; postittaa
matches tulitikkuja
medium keskikoko
menu ruokalista
message viesti
museum museo

N

nail (body) kynsi
nail clippers kynsileikkuri
nail file kynsiviila
nail salon kynsihoitola
name nimi
napkin lautasliina
nurse sairaanhoitaja

O

o'clock kello
occupation ammatti
occupied varattu
office toimisto
off-licence [BE] viinakauppa; Alko **(the chain in Finland)**
or tai
orange (color) oranssi

P

pacifier (baby's) tutti
packet paketti
park *n ; v* puisto; pysäköidä
pen kynä
pink vaaleanpunainen **(light pink)**; pinkki **(bright pink)**
plate lautanen
please ole hyvä
plug (electric) pistoke
purple purppuranpunainen

Q

quality laatu
quantity määrä
question *n* kysymys
quick nopea(sti)
quiet hiljainen

R

race kilpailu
racket (sport) maila
railway station [BE] rautatieasema
rain sade
raincoat sadetakki
rape *n* raiskaus
razor (disposable) (kertakäyttöisen) partaterän
razor blade partaterä
red punainen
room (hotel); (space) huone; tila
room service huonepalvelu

S

safe *n* **(vault) ; (not in danger)** tallelokero; turvallinen

safety pin hakaneula
sailboat purjehdusvene
sale *n* ; **(bargains)** myynti; alennusmyynti
same sama(nlainen)
sand hiekka
salty suolaista
sandal sandaali
sanitary napkin terveysside
sauna sauna
scissors sakset
Scotland Skotlanti
shampoo/conditioner šampoota/hoitoainetta
shoe kenkä
small pieni
sneaker lenkkitossu
snow lumi
soap saippua
sock sukka
spicy foods tulisia ruokia
spoon lusikka
stamp *n* **(postage)** ; *v* **(ticket)** postimerkki; leimata
suitcase matkalaukku
sun aurinko
sunglasses aurinkolasit
sun-tan lotion aurinkovoide
sweater neulepusero
sweatshirt college-pusero
swimsuit uimapuku

T

table pöytä
tablet (medical) tabletti

take ottaa
take away *v* **[BE]** ottaa mukaan
tampon tamponi
terrible kamala
thank you kiitos
ticket lippu
tie solmio
tissue nenäliina
toilet paper WC-paperi
toothbrush hammasharja
toothpaste hammastahna
tough sitkeää
toy lelu
T-shirt t-paita

U

ugly ruma
umbrella ; (beach) sateenvarjo; aurinkovarjo
unconscious tajuton
under alla, alle
underground station [BE] metroasema
underwear alusvaatteet
United States Yhdysvallat
university yliopisto

V

vacancy vapaa huone
vacant vapaa
vacation loma
vaccinate rokottaa
vegan vegaani
vegetarian kasvissyöjä

W

wait *v* odottaa
waiter tarjoilija
waiting room odotushuone
waitress tarjoilija
waterfall vesiputous
waterproof vedenkestävä
weather forecast sääennuste
week viikko
weekend viikonloppu
white valkoinen
wife vaimo
with kanssa
without ilman

X

X-ray röntgen

Y

yacht huvipursi
year vuosi
yellow keltainen
yes kyllä
yesterday eilen
yet vielä
young nuori
youth hostel nuorisohostelli

Z

zero nolla
zoo eläintarha

Berlitz®

speaking your language

phrase book & dictionary
phrase book & CD

Available in: Arabic, Brazilian Portuguese*, Burmese*, Cantonese
Chinese, Croatian, Czech*, Danish*, Dutch, English, Filipino, Finnish*, French,
German, Greek, Hebrew*, Hindi*, Hungarian*, Indonesian, Italian, Japanese,
Korean, Latin American Spanish, Malay, Mandarin Chinese, Mexican Spanish,
Norwegian, Polish, Portuguese, Romanian*, Russian, Spanish, Swedish, Thai,
Turkish, Vietnamese
*Book only